LEGACY

Ancient Philosophy for Modern Minds

PHIL QUIRK

Published: June 2022 by FCM Publishing

ISBN: 9781914529368 Paperback
ISBN: 9781914529375 eBook

Cover Design by Danji's Designs

DEDICATION

For my wild and beautiful daughters Aalin & Nancy. I wrote this book to inspire you both now and in the future; you are my universe and I hope this book inspires you both.

Learn like you might live forever, live like you might die tomorrow.

For my life's inspiration, Ruth. Your philosophy of life has furnished my life beyond any words I could hope to write. You are the hero of this story and the living embodiment of much of this book.

ACKNOWLEDGEMENTS

There are so many people to thank who have contributed to this book.

I would like to firstly acknowledge the philosophers and thinkers who's ideas are the bedrock of this book. For Mick and the wider Omnia Mind team who turn my ideas into something real outside of my head.

Andy, Claudia, Alec (and Alec's parents), Ruth who were all marvellous proof readers and soundboards. My business partner Mark for pushing me hard to write, and especially for Andy MT who was a consistent source of encouragement, and oc-casional harassment. Finally, I'd like to sincerely thank Taryn and her team at FCM for taking on a book about an-cient philosophy in the modern world.

Contents

Synopsis

The process of developing the minds and bodies of Spartan youths to eventually become warriors was called the Agoge. During the Agoge, young Spartans would undertake challenges, experience adversity, build resilience, sharpen their thoughts, and forge their self-reliance. The ancient Spartans knew that to create the fierce warriors they craved, they had to endow the most indefatigable mindset possible. The world we live in today is far removed from Spartan culture; modernity has shaped our society, and our evolution has provided comfort and abundance unimaginable to our ancestors. There have been unforeseen consequences from the advancement born from the seeds of agriculture, nurtured by industrialism, and accelerated by technology. Rarely throughout history has mankind experienced such collective comfort, yet also paradoxically experiencing rising levels of both anxiety and depression. According to the 2017 global survey conducted by Deloite, mental illness has rapidly and relentlessly unfolded itself onto a technologically distracted human race, like a foreboding tidal surge strands those unaware of its advancement. Human evolution and modernity will not relent from this perilous point in time, the prizes are too great and the consequences of falling behind other nations will possibly accelerate us into oblivion.

Maybe we're not living longer, maybe we're just taking longer to die.

Something needs to change because something is most certainly not working in our evolved societies. The starting point might be revisiting the wisdom and knowledge handed down from the ancients, often cast aside with the emergence of new 'shiny' concepts. The legacy they leave behind is in plain sight yet unnoticed by the digital age. Drawing upon my service in the elite Royal Marines Commandos, and latterly my career as a world-class Human Performance Coach, I share the ideas and philosophies that have enabled me to help thousands of my clients achieve and surpass their desired goals.

No quick fixes, no gimmicks, no snake oil. It is the philosophy of applying knowledge daily and repeatedly with relentless commitment.

Legacy: Ancient Philosophy for Modern Minds, is a book that draws upon ideas, knowledge and wisdom over a significant epoch in human history. From 2,500-year-old ancient Greek Stoic Philosophy to modern theories about the mindset of our human species, I leave no stone unturned in the pursuit of the most important of all knowledge – the wisdom of 'knowing thyself'. This book has 99 unique ideas distilled into short chapters that can be read individually or sequentially, with most chapters containing practical applications.

The goal of my book is straightforward and bold: learn from past wisdom to think more effectively today.

Socrates, Marcus Aurelius, Zeno, Seneca, Da Vinci, Sir Isaac Newton, Sylvester Stallone, Thales, Plato, and Forrest Gump all contribute their philosophies to build a compelling mindset manifesto for the future of our modern species.

Preface

Welcome to the start of a journey we shall undertake together. My intention for writing this book was relatively simple; to empower you to make some positive changes, improve your mindset, and perhaps ignite your passion and curiosity for ancient knowledge such as Greek Philosophy and the Spartan Agoge. Maybe the most crucial element of this book is to encourage you to accept adversity into your life. This is not a book about happiness, instead it is a working manual for developing resilience, temperance, and resolve that you can apply in any area of your life. It would be foolish of me to make bold claims about the results you might experience reading this book – that will depend largely on your application of these ancient ideas. The critical component is turning these ideas into daily actions and habits.

I certainly cannot, nor will not, guarantee that once you have finished reading, you'll have the tools to manifest a mansion, a new Ferrari complete with cliched swimming pool for social media, nor will these pages multiply your earning power by ten. What I can boldly claim, however, is if you complete this book you'll become intellectually, spiritually and philosophically wealthier. Should this be the outcome of our 'hero's journey' then I shall be both proud and happy, for this book will have realised my hopes, and perhaps much more.

This book is not about self-help, nor is it written with any therapeutic intention; it is more accurately about self-education and self-development. Throughout the book, there are fundamental themes drawn from various bodies of knowledge that have shaped my coaching philosophy. These great thinkers and philosophers have without doubt shaped my mind, and I hope I can pass this knowledge forward to you. The blend of these theories and philosophies has enabled me to write this book. To achieve this I have 'stood on the shoulders of giants' for my inspiration. Specifically I take my knowledge from Stoicism and other Greek Philosophies, as well as Positive Psychology, Hypnosis, Neurolinguistic Programming (NLP), and various forms of Breathwork including Breatheology, Pranayama, the Wim Hof Method, and Holotropic Breathing.

It has taken me many years to develop my mindset. Researching and writing this book has brought these concepts and philosophies sharply into the focus. From a personal perspective, this process alone has been incredibly refreshing, and somewhat cathartic. I cast my mind back to the times I have lived through adversity and how the application of these concepts served me well, both at the time and in reflection afterwards.

During my career I have worked with and studied high performers such as UK and US Special Forces, Olympic and World champion athletes, Polar explorers, Fast Jet Pilots, and entrepreneurs. The book is written in short chapters with each chapter representing an idea, concept, or philosophy. It is written this way so you can explore the book non-sequentially. Because of this, you can pick the book up from any page and read a chapter without the need to follow a linear approach.

My vision for this book is to help you develop your knowledge, improve your resilience levels, change your limiting beliefs, and become more self-reflective in the process. I genuinely hope to impart as much of my knowledge and experience over the coming chapters as I can, and I encourage you to pass these ideas on should they resonate with you at any level.

Within this book I also introduce you to the idea of the Spartan Agoge. The Agoge were the trials young Spartan boys set out upon at an early age to develop their resilience, self-belief, fortitude and self-reliance – all qualities worthy of pursuit today. You have been on your Agoge since childhood, perhaps without realising it consciously. I urge you to intentionally take control of your Agoge and reap the rewards from this pursuit of resilience.

Much of the success of this book resides in the action you commit with each concept. It is not enough to learn and absorb the knowledge without practically applying it to your day-to-day life, and this is another reason each chapter is short in length to encourage action from you.

INTRODUCTION

Acknowledge That All Emotions Come From Within

"Between stimulus and response, there is a space. In that space is our power to choose our response. In our response lies our growth and our freedom."
– *Viktor E. Frankl*

We begin our exploration of Stoicism, philosophy, and mindset principles in the German concentration camps of World War 2. Viktor Frankl was an Austrian born psychiatrist, philosopher, author and Holocaust survivor. During his incarceration in Auschwitz and Dachau between 1942 and 1945, Viktor Frankl endured almost unimaginable physical, psychological, and spiritual torture. He embodied many of Stoicism's core principles, and we need to look no further than his eloquent, yet powerful words to start this journey.

Many of my clients have very much been prisoners of their minds and emotions. I have also shared this mental incarceration during my teenage years, as well as from time to time as an adult. Quietly, I have always held the belief that as a teenager I experienced periods of non-diagnosed depression. Often, without reason, I would find myself thinking unwanted thoughts, sometimes entertaining suicide ideation. It was as if I had somehow contracted a cognitive virus that contaminated my internal thoughts. At times it felt as if my mind was a double agent, sometimes working for the good of me and other times wickedly conspiring my demise. I can never be confident of an accurate diagnosis, mainly because I chose not to share these experiences at the time, preferring to find ways to conceal my inner feelings and thoughts with surprising ease from the outside world.

Two things were certain though. Firstly, I was a prisoner inside my mind and enslaved to my emotions. Secondly, I learned that everything started and ended in my mind.

The situation came to a head around 1994, when I was in my final few high school years. At the time, I was experiencing a certain amount of depression, predominately caused by an episode of bullying at school combined with my grandfather's passing the year prior. My grandfather's passing had profoundly affected me, although I was working astutely to conceal this. Without doubt, he was a significant influence on my life until his death in the summer of 1993, and it is still difficult to verbalise the immense feeling of loss I felt. I had always despised school and considered myself a slight misfit, not insomuch as I did not have friends, but more accurately I did not have close friends, preferring to drift aimlessly from group to group.

The depression I was experiencing, mainly due to my circumstance, was steadily coming to a head. With this perfect emotional storm brewing, I made the desperate decision to take my own life. This regretful action is something I have felt an immense sense of shame for, primarily because I do not believe I wanted to die. I just yearned for my circumstances to be different and wanted to relieve the feeling of endless hopelessness I had cultivated internally for many months. I think suicide is still very much a taboo topic, and I believe we are nowhere near the point of bringing the subject out of the shadows into open conversation. I cannot recall a more awkward conversation in my life than the one with the vicar and my parents as I lay in the hospital bed. Once discharged from the hospital, it was never mentioned within my family again. I had made my mind up as I lay in the hospital bed at the age of fifteen: I needed to be more robust of mind and body and the seeds for the Royal Marines were sown during my weakest point in life.

My entire drive for joining the Royal Marines in 1998 at the age of twenty was to strengthen my mind, improve my slender physique, and establish some respect from my family and friends. Perhaps, most importantly, I wanted to prove people wrong. In truth, I achieved none of these things as a Royal Marine Commando. It took me many years to work out the salvation of my mind lay in self-education and learning, not needless peacock feathering. It took me several more years to let go of the desire to exchange external achievement for recognition and respect. If you don't respect yourself, nobody else will regardless of the accolades, achievements, and awards.

Once I had joined the Royal Marines, the attempted suicide seemed to belong to a different life altogether. It had become resigned to the deepest recesses of my mind and in all honesty, I didn't give it much thought at all. By the time I had reached my late 20s, I decided to leave the Royal Marines and join the Royal Air Force as a Physical Training Instructor (PTI). Once I'd reached the milestone of thirty years old in the RAF, it almost felt as if the suicide attempt never happened at all – out of sight out of mind. This strategy had served me well for many years until I began the journey inside my thoughts to unpick some of the unhelpful beliefs forged throughout adolescence.

By the age of thirty I had decided to become a mindset coach, this presented me with a completely different dilemma to wrestle with. At the start of my career, I did not want to openly express the desperate decision I had made as a teenager. I regretted my actions as fifteen-year-old and feared being judged unfit to coach. Once I had become relatively successful as a professional coach I was presented with an opposing problem. At this stage it became difficult to broach the subject out of fear of possible accusations of opportunism and jumping on the 'mental health bandwagon' to further myself professionally. I had unwittingly dug myself into a pit of silence and secrecy and spoke to very few people about that time of my life. This is the first time since 1994 I have shared these events publicly.

In January 2017 one of my closest friends, Andrew 'Mozzer' Morris, tragically took his own life. It completely devastated me for several reasons. Firstly, and by far the most painful, was the overwhelming feeling of sorrow and shame for my inability to help him. By 2017 I had coached many people successfully and being unable to offer any meaningful help to Moz made me feel an intense anger towards myself. It tortured me. When news started to spread via social media of Mozzer's passing, I was in northern Sweden, working with another close friend, Matt. Being in the wilderness was a blessing in many ways, and it was truly the best place on earth I could have been to receive such devastating news. The raw expanse of the Swedish wilderness, coupled with being around Matt, as well as the group we were working with, softened the blow. It almost felt unreal at that point, and I dealt with the news calmly, professionally, and objectively. My ability to cope with the situation was perhaps aided by being able to focus my mind on completing the work with Matt, which was both physically and mentally challenging. However, the calm focus I experienced in Sweden quickly changed on arrival back in the UK. My immediate reaction on landing was to travel to South Wales and meet with Adam King, or 'Kingy' as we all know him by (there were four of us who were incredibly close, Kahmeel Spence being the final member of our quartet). What ensued was a drinking session that began in Abergavenny and continued to Manchester, before finally moving south to Falmouth in Cornwall for the funeral.

Mozzer's funeral was a blur. I was drinking before the church; the self-justification to do so is easy under such circumstances. The downward spiral had begun. For several months after the funeral, I descended into a bottomless hole of self-pity, fuelled by my relentless drinking sessions. Most of the time I was in London creating the illusion of 'busyness' by pretending to attend fictitious meetings or working out of our office in central London. In fact, I was drinking every day. I believe that pity is one of the most dangerous and addictive emotions created in the human consciousness. Filled with this self-pity, guilt, and self-loathing, I didn't want to be near anyone. Similar to my earlier experiences concealing my true feelings as a teenager, once again it was frightening the ease with which I could convince others that all was fine, when internally all I wanted to do was end the conversation or phone call as fast as possible to start (or carry on) with my alcohol fuelled madness uninterrupted.

After nine or ten weeks, I started taking action; choosing small, positive decisions and moving away from all of the destructive choices I had made during the previous few months. To climb out of a deep hole, the first task is to put the shovel down. In my case the shovel was alcohol, and I wasn't very far away from being too deep. Thankfully, I was able to climb out, but I am very aware that others are not so lucky. Because of this I have always reserved as much empathy as I can for people struggling with any substance addiction.

Many of the chapters of this book were enjoyable, cathartic, educational and sometimes even therapeutic to create. I have learned unequivocally, throughout both personal experiences, that all of my emotions and feelings exist only within myself. With this at the forefront of my thoughts, I know I have a responsibility to take care of my mind and body, which gives me the best chance of choosing my positive reactions.

So today is the start of a 99-chapter journey we walk together. Each chapter will be short and to the point using Greek Philosophy (specifically Stoicism), elements of Psychology and a little bit of science, interspersed with mindset tips and metaphors developed through my professional journey in performance coaching. These ideas should challenge and arrest your perceptions of yourself, encouraging you to think beyond your biases and develop the fortitude and resilience necessary to thrive in our modern society. From whichever point you start on this journey, always hold the end in mind and focus on your outcome. Commitment always overcomes motivation, because commitment is unwavering and resolute, like the famous Greek Stoics. It all starts and finishes between your ears and the number one priority for us all should be how to use our minds more effectively.

Between the stimulus and responses of life, we are presented the opportunity to choose our reactions; this responsibility lies within us all.

It all starts and ends in the minds of man.

"A dog starved at the master's gate predicts
the ruin of the state."
– Blake

CHAPTER 1

Stoicism Virtue 1/4 – Wisdom

"To be ever minded is the greatest virtue."
*– **Heraclitus***

Virtue is described as "behaviour showing high morals". The Greek Stoic philosophers held four virtues above everything else, and with an additional set of principles these form the concept of Stoicism. Throughout this book, we will explore the four virtues as well as the principles in various chapters.

Wisdom is the first virtue, and it seems appropriate we start the book with this critical virtue to build everything else upon. I have often thought about wisdom and wondered how it differs to knowledge. In truth, they are connected, but perhaps not synonymous. The Collins dictionary defines wisdom as "the ability to discern or judge what is true, right, or lasting". However, knowledge is referred to as "information gained through experience, reasoning, or acquaintance".

Knowledge can be present without wisdom, but wisdom can only be found in the wake of knowledge. It is like the symbiotic relationship between a parent and child. An adult can exist childless, but a child cannot exist without first the adult.

Knowledge opens the door to wisdom.

I have met many knowledgeable people throughout my life's journey, however, encounters of true wisdom have been much less frequent. It is as if the evolution of wisdom from knowledge is the frontier explored outside of the structure of lessons and classrooms, and without academic texts. Wisdom requires the knowledge of 'how' something works but more importantly, the subjective judgement of 'when' to use it, which cannot be acquired so easily.

For example: you may know how to use hypnosis; it is not a particularly difficult subject to learn the basics of. Still, the real skill lies within the wisdom of knowing when to use a specific technique or approach, at an undisclosed and subjective point in time with a client who is entirely unique. Walking the path of knowledge is a much shorter and well-documented journey than the path to wisdom; perhaps this is why so many people retire content after arriving at 'knowing'?

Think about the elements of your life you might consider yourself knowledgeable in and ask yourself the following questions in search for the presence of wisdom:

"Is this only knowledge I possess? Is there also wisdom within the knowledge of this subject?"

Reflection: Wisdom is achieved by combining knowledge and experience, supplemented with constant reflection. The pursuit is always to 'know thyself' a little more each day. Consider taking some of the learning from these pages and applying it to your day-to-day life while still affording yourself the time and space for reflection. Once you reach the point of mastery through commitment and thought, pass the knowledge and wisdom you have acquired to those around you.

"Those that know, do. Those that understand, teach."
– Aristotle

CHAPTER 2

Quit Quitting

"Look well into thyself; there is a source of strength which will always spring up if thou wilt always look."
– Marcus Aurelius

Marcus Aurelius was a renowned Stoic and his seminal book *Meditations* is still revered today, nearly 2,000 years after it was initially penned. In this modern world of comfort and abundance, we can learn so much from the ideas, principles and concepts Marcus Aurelius describes within his writings. Our ancestors of antiquity wrestled with challenges we have long forgotten, like the ongoing struggle of survival in a sometimes primitive and harsh world. The ancients certainly would not be able to work a modern phone, but equally, how would a modern human fare when asked to start a fire without matches? In many ways, we have evolved our intelligence, but we have also *devolved* in other areas. We have undoubtedly become much lazier of thought. Over time we have surrendered some of our critical thinking at the accessible altar of modernity and now occupy an unusual human evolution paradox. In many respects, we are far superior to the ancient philosophers that I consistently turn to within these pages, however, I believe we are intellectually inferior as a collective species. Simply observing our modern handwriting and the application of language in both the written and spoken form compared to that of our ancestors speaks volumes about the devolution of both of these skills. We are undoubtedly less able and competent in graphology as well as the spoken word than previously in history. Technology precludes us the mundanity of having to think deeply or remember information that we can access at the speed of internet connection bandwidth.

"Understand at last that you have something in you more powerful and divine than what causes the bodily passions and pulls you like a mere puppet. What thoughts now occupy my mind? Is it not fear, suspicion, desire, or something like that?"
– Marcus Aurelius

What the great Roman emperor is saying within this quote is that the thoughts that pull our mind in different directions are often unchallenged and unexamined. One of Stoicism's principles is to develop an even mind that neither participates in catastrophe or unfounded elation. It is the fundamental acceptance that nothing is permanent; joy gives way in the same that pain subsides over time – the only permanent thing is change.

Reflection: Our thoughts can pull us from side to side and back and forth. The unexamined mind can be a precariously fickle pilot of our internal thinking, and time drags us into destructive patterns of thought. Taking control of your thoughts will enable you to assert more control over your day-to-day wellbeing, which will dramatically improve your life. The key is to keep moving forward, little by little each day, even at a sometimes unperceivable amount, in order to make progress. Take quitting out of the equation; see this task through to its full completion. As the incredible Nimsdai Purja said on his way to conquering all fourteen of the world's 8,000m peaks in less than seven months; "Sometimes when you feel you are fucked, you are only about 45% fucked!" Objectivity is the key to gaining control of your thoughts.

"Never discourage anyone who continually makes progress, no matter how slow."

– Plato

CHAPTER 3

Back Yourself

"He who sees things grow from the beginning will have the best view of them."
– Aristotle

Many people widely acknowledge Tom Brady as one of the greatest American football players of all time, and most certainly the greatest ever quarterback. Brady has won the Super Bowl an almost unbelievable seven times, six times with the New England Patriots and once with the Tampa Bay Buccaneers. Such is Brady's success he has won the Super Bowl more times as an individual (seven) than any single team (six). His accolades list could fill this entire book, and there are undoubtedly many books that have paid homage to his unrivalled athletic achievements.

What isn't so well known is Brady's early career and his 2000 draft performance.

Brady was below average in every physical measurement. The National Football League (NFL) utilises a weeklong event called 'the combine', which is a set of standardised physical tests to ascertain the athletic capability of a player. The combine consists of the 40-yard dash, bench press (225 lb repetitions), vertical jump, broad jump, 20-yard shuttle, 3-cone drill, 60-yard shuttle, and position-specific drills. The 40-yard dash is a particular benchmark of general athletic ability and Brady's time of 5.28 seconds is still one of the slowest recorded by any quarterback in recent memory. In every one of the tests, Brady's scores were at best forgettable. Added to this, his gawky and somewhat awkward NFL picture in only his shorts, embodied anything but a future Hall of Famer.

Consequentially, Brady had to wait until the 7th round of the draft, as the 199th pick and 7th choice quarterback. Twenty-one years after the now-infamous 2000 draft, and with seven Super Bowl victories to his name, Tom Brady must go down in history as the greatest failure in modern sport.

For us all there is a starting point in every situation, the first step towards a goal is always the farthest from the end. The stadium-filling band that rehearses terribly for the very first time, the Michelin starred chef who picks up a knife for the first time, and the greatest ever NFL quarterbacks' first time holding a football; they all started with the first step.

The first person to believe in your success is you, and long before the accolades return from virtuous performances you have to back yourself, maybe even at times when no one else backs you. It is easier said than done, that is for certain. Believing in yourself when you seem miles away from any future success is not simple or straightforward. Still, if you have enough passion, dedication and commitment, success will most certainly follow in time.

Reflection: Could you imagine what Tom Brady thought after posting his combine score? Is it possible to consider what his thought process was as six quarterbacks were picked before him in the 2000 NFL draft? I can only wonder how it would have felt for 198 players to be selected ahead of him. What did that do to his confidence?

Talent is, without doubt, a factor in defining success in any area, but it is not *the* critical component. Dedication, application, and commitment are essential elements, and all of these are mental applications, not physical.

If you want others to back you in this world, you first have to back yourself.

CHAPTER 4

Who's Driving the Ship?

"From the very beginning, make it your practice to say to every harsh situation, 'You are an impression and not at all what you appear to be.' Next, examine and test it by the rules you possess, the first and greatest of which is this – whether it belongs to the things in our control or not in our control, and if the latter, be prepared to respond with, 'This is nothing to me.'"

– ***Epictetus***

Who's the captain of your ship?

Have you ever considered why some things can draw a reaction from you, while other situations can pass you by unbothered? Do you choose your response in accordance with the way you want to react, or are you the reactionary cart tied inextricably to the horse of emotion? Do you perceive these reactions as the result of your conscious mind or unconscious mind; is there an awareness present?

When are you at *cause* and when does causation become *effect*? Does the event precipitate the reaction or is the reaction a preconscious catalyst for the event itself?

When I coach, I often gift my clients a book at the start of their coaching journey; the book is Viktor Frankl's seminal *Man's Search for Meaning*. I give this book for two unconnected reasons. Firstly, I want them to commit to action between our sessions; if they do not start reading the book between sessions, we can discuss their commitment to change. Secondly, I believe that *Man's Search for Meaning* represents one of the most outstanding books ever written to understand the elementary human choices we have in any given situation, regardless of circumstance, suffering or despair. The book is set against the backdrop of the Nazi run Auschwitz and Dachau concentration camps and details the almost unimaginable brutality suffered there during World War 2. Dr Frankl draws incredible observations and subsequent conclusions about the human mind and body's indomitable spirit and resilience.

Frankl writes about the desire to hold onto his last freedom – the ability to choose his reaction in any given situation, regardless of the external conditions. He believed that whatever the Nazis took from him, or did to him, he could make a conscious choice, which led to his reaction to the situation. The *effect* was not pre-determined by the *cause*. This *last free-*

dom gave him a purpose in a reality that was very much without many, if any, positives. As he wonderfully penned: "a person with a *why* can overcome any *what*".

Reflection: Consider the last time you lost your temper. Now consider how, once calmed down, you perhaps thought very differently about the situation. Had you the ability to jump forward in time to the calmer 'state' of thinking, would you have acted differently? Of course, this is not always easy to practically apply, but with perseverance and temperance, these reactions can be overridden with the response you would prefer to choose. We still have choices available to us in any scenario or situation and pursuing the mindset that enables you to select your reaction will reap incredible rewards in the future. The captain never chooses the weather but he no doubt influences the outcome of the storm with his actions.

"In a position of utter desolation, when man cannot express himself in positive action, when his only achievement may consist in enduring his sufferings in the right way – an honourable way – in such a position man can, through loving contemplation of the image he carries of his beloved, achieve fulfilment."

– Viktor Frankl

CHAPTER 5

No Harm, No Foul

"Do away with the opinion I am harmed, and the harm is cast away too. Do away with being harmed, and harm disappears too."

– Marcus Aurelius

What if I was to make the following statement? "Your perception of me is a projection of you; my reaction to you is an awareness of me."

Take a few moments to run these words through your mind, exploring what the statement creates. What might you interpret as the 'meaning' behind this statement?

We are by our very evolutionary nature meaning-seeking creatures, which might explain our desire to align ourselves with various religions throughout history.

We yearn to *belong* almost as much as we crave to know how things *end*, and perhaps more importantly, what comes after the *end*? These are all existential questions that have vexed and perplexed our most celebrated and enigmatic thinkers throughout the history of man. They are also *loosely* answered in various religious texts. Providing us with these conclusions affords us peace of mind and permits a sense of certainty to continue with life in accordance with the rule of the book. As long as these rules are assiduously adhered to, safe onward passage through seraphic gates will be our reward at the final reckoning.

Since the dawn of time, this final reward has been the divine promise and roughly consistent with nearly all religions, regardless of geographical or temporal origin.

In truth, there is no subjective meaning to anything, until we give it meaning via our consciousness. I ascribe meaning to the words of religious texts through the prismatic influences of my values and beliefs. A dog observes the writings of a *King James Bible* or *The Holy Qur'an* with same indifference as if it were to look at a copy of the *Yellow Pages*. It is not my place for one second to question either religious text; it is merely to observe that the meaning of both is wholly reliant on the reader's emotional processing and subjective interpretation.

Reality happens around us, and when we observe this through our five fundamental senses, we then attach meaning to these external events. We see, hear, feel, smell and taste our outer reality, we then ascribe meaning to these events via unconscious filtering. Before *observation,* these events hold no subjective meaning, but once *observed* objectivity is transformed wondrously into subjectivity. We are then free to attach importance to any event once this principle is understood. This is because we are influenced beneath our conscious awareness by our subconscious judgements, biases, values and beliefs.

We observe the world through a lens, and this can behave much more as a prism to reality than a lens. Because of this we 'see' the world as 'we' see it, not necessarily how it is.

Reflection: The lens through which you observe your reality defines the meaning you give to your reality. Each of us filters experience subjectively and no two people see the same reality. Once you become aware that you're viewing a distorted perspective of the world *outside,* it gives you the unique opportunity to focus on the world *inside,* which is where all of your reactions reside. Grasping your reactions starts with first understanding your perceptions.

CHAPTER 6

Today IS the Day!

"A man who dares to waste one hour of time has not discovered the value of life."
– Charles Darwin

Forrest Gump once declared, "Life is like a box of chocolates", according to his momma. For me, life is less like a box of chocolates and more like a box of matches.

Imagine your life as a metaphorical box of matches; each match represents each single day of your life. Every match is ignited one at a time and sequentially, you only ever have the light from the single match you hold. This brings your life to *light* with the present moment. We generally don't know when the last match will be taken from the box and struck, although we might occasionally be aware of the box running out.

What do you intend to do with today's light?

Through many years of helping people with their mindset, I've realised that most humans rarely appreciate the match they hold in their hand. Much of the context of our lives is predicated on looking toward the future. Most people are paid their salary monthly (or occasionally weekly), so often look forward to the end of the month when they get paid. For many, there's often too much month left at the end of the money. We focus on how it will feel going on our yearly holiday and ponder the often only annual event throughout the year. We're always busy going somewhere, meeting someone (later), or preparing the report for next week. Now don't get me wrong, in certain ways we are pre-conditioned for this – consider the Christmas advent calendar you might have excitedly opened each day as a child.

It is partly because of this future-focused conditioning we often don't notice what's happening ***now***!

What are the sounds happening around you as you read this page? What sensations can you feel, either internally or externally, that perhaps you weren't paying attention to before you read these words? What are you missing right now, by being overly focused on later? What can you start to pay closer attention to in this single, precious, eternal *now*?

"I don't complain about the lack of time... what little I have will go far enough. Today – this day – will achieve what no tomorrow will fail to speak about. I will lay siege to the Gods and shake up the world!"

– ***Seneca***

We may very well all start from various elevation points in life, but our account with time is equal, regardless of wealth, status, or geography. The difference is often the metaphor for which we ascribe to time; do you 'waste' it, maybe 'kill' it, or perhaps 'spend' it? There seems to be very few that 'invest' their time, in my experience.

Reflection: The use of your time allocated will be the ultimate measure of your life. When you take the final match out from the box, how many matches will you reflect as wasted? How many people would exchange all of their wealth for just a few more matches at the end?

Unfortunately, there are no re-runs or refunds; we have our allocation of matches but have no prescription of what to do with them. It is up to us all as individuals to be studious and wise in applying ourselves during each of these precious days. Use your match wisely today.

CHAPTER 7

Perfection Is the Enemy of Action

"We don't abandon our pursuits because we despair of ever perfecting them."
– ***Epictetus***

The thing with perfection is it can sabotage the real jewel: progression. Perfection rarely exists outside the universal and omnipotent wand of Mother Nature, but it doesn't stop us trying to run towards the *perfection horizon* nonetheless. It probably wouldn't surprise you to learn this perfection horizon causes both premature abandonment and outright despair. Rather than aim for perfection at some far away unassigned point in the future, aim for progression today.

As James Clear brilliantly writes in his remarkable book *Atomic Habits*, "If for every day you awoke and achieved a 1% improvement in an area of your life, at the end of that year you would be 37.78 times better than the start." Imagine being 37.78 times better at something in only one year!

Perfection has also incurred another tax on the history of human productivity. How many things haven't you started because you're just not 'good' at them? I have numerous friends, and many clients, who have '*wanted*' to start something, stop something, or change something, or a combination of any of these. The common denominator for the lack of action in all three areas is imperfection paralysis. If your perception is that you're not good at something, then it is safer never to try and avoid the potential public shaming of your ability. This is the gap that exists between *wanting* and *doing*.

Another gap exists between *knowing* and *doing* and this can often be the most significant chasm to cross before action. Most people know that exercise is good for them, they know what a good diet consists of, and they know that practising mindfulness will improve their mental wellbeing. Why then do so few people continuously adhere to these positive pursuits? I may be aware of my desire to learn a new language, but if paralysed by inaction, the language will always be resigned to something I wish I'd done.

When is the best time to plant an oak tree? Twenty years ago!

When is the next best time to plant an oak tree? Today.

The challenge in the world is rarely information, more often it is implementation.

We can often think in a very binary way and the extremity of polar contrast. Things are either entirely north, or south. You're either with me or against me. Anything less than absolute success is a failure. I can either speak Spanish or cannot. Thinking in this binary way, we discard the considerable space between the poles where progression resides.

Reflection: Instead of thinking in such black or white contrasts, see instead the grey in between. This perspective will develop temperance to your thinking. Learning a new language takes time and perseverance, it doesn't happen without these two ingredients. Fundamentally, this is why many people either never start the task or abandon before they see significant improvement. This is referred to as the 'valley of disappointment' which shows us that initial progress is rarely as substantial as imagined, leading to abandoning the project with the reinforced belief that learning a new language, for example, is outside of their capability. In reality, they just didn't persevere to the point of desired results. Get started, start progressing, maintain. Become a *'progressionist'.*

CHAPTER 8

Fail We May, Sail We Must

This chapter's title is one of my favourite quotes, taken from the late, great, musical maverick Andrew Weatherall. There is always the chance of failure in everything we participate in. Everyday life presents us with the opportunity for failure. From the moment we wake to the moment we slip back into sleep, we navigate the tightrope between success and failure, perhaps even failing in the pursuit of sleep, as insomniacs know only too well. However, the possibility of failure should never discourage the attempt for that would be the only true and absolute failure.

"Ships in the harbour are safe, but that's not what they are built for."
– Albert Einstein

Humans can be a little like the ships Einstein describes. We yearn for the harbour's safety but also wonder about the adventures that await us on the expansive ocean. Fear can cripple humans and does so frequently. Fear disguises itself as inactivity and apathy; it is a much easier decision to choose safety before danger. And if given the option, most humans will enthusiastically choose the safe known, before the dangerous unknown; we're just hardwired this way.

The key to leaving the harbour is practising temperance and utilising the gift of acceptance and surrender. You may fail in what you undertake, but there is infinitely more success in trying and not succeeding than in never having tried at all. You cannot control the storm of the ocean outside, but your reaction to the storm is within your wheelhouse and well within your circle of influence. This is, without doubt, the measure of your character.

I often notice this when observing clients enter into the merciless cold water for the first time. Many are too afraid even to attempt it and dismiss their capability from the outset resigning themselves to such limiting language as, "I could never do that!" Or worse still, "That's impossible!"

Those that overcome this often try to fight the cold with anger, aggression, and determination. You cannot fight cold any more than you can land a clean punch square on the chin of a gust of wind. In truth, all you can ever do is surrender to the strength of nature, and in doing so, you immediately align yourself with its power.

"Empty your mind, be formless, shapeless — like water. Now you put water in a cup; it becomes the cup. You put water into a bottle; it becomes the bottle; You put it in a teapot; it becomes the teapot. Now water can flow, or it can crash. Be water, my friend."

– ***Bruce Lee***

Reflection: The thing you've wanted to do but the timing has never been quite right – the language you wanted to learn, a hobby you wanted to start, the marathon you wanted to enter – start it right now. Not next week or even tomorrow – right now! Accept the storms that will surely come and focus only on your response. The storm itself is not your responsibility, but your reaction to it is yours.

Leave the harbour, you're meant for bigger things!

"It is not death that a man should fear, but he should fear never beginning to live."

– ***Marcus Aurelius***

CHAPTER 9

The Wolf You Feed

"We do not inherit the earth from our ancestors; we borrow it from our children."

– Cherokee Proverb

One evening an old Cherokee chief told his grandson about the battle that rages within us all. He said; "My son, there is a battle which rages inside you; it is a battle between two wolves. These wolves fight every day to take control of your soul. One wolf is evil; it is anger, envy, regret, jealousy, doubt, greed, arrogance, self-pity, guilt, resentment, false pride, and superiority. The other wolf is good. It has joy, peace, love, happiness, sincerity, humility, kindness, benevolence, empathy, generosity, forgiveness, compassion, faith, and truth. These two wolves fight day after day to take control of the character and spirit of each one of us."

The grandson considered the words of his grandfather for a while before looking deep into his eyes and asking, "Grandfather, how will I know which wolf will win?"

The old chief simply replied, "It will be the one you choose to feed the most."

Inside us resides the potential to do good and the potential for evil at the same time. Consider all the good things you have ever done against all the wrong things. Consider the times when you have been proud of your actions, against the times when, uncomfortably, you fell short of your moral compass. You're the same person throughout the entirety of your behaviour, but your behaviour can move and change from moment to moment, situation to situation, and time to time. You are sometimes swinging from one polarity to the other.

Which wolf do you feed the most and with which wolf are you most familiar?

The Greek Stoics can teach us much about how we choose to behave in any given situation or moment. The ability to select our behaviour deliberately is not assumed an easy skill without practice. How many times have you chosen the wrong action, in the wrong context, at the wrong time? For many of the philosophers of antiquity, mastery of these virtues represented their entire life's pursuit.

Reflection: One way to start controlling your reactions and behaviour is to ask yourself some logical questions that redirect the neural activity from your emotional limbic brain, into your more reasoned and rational frontal cortex.

"Will I regret this behaviour in an hour once I've reflected on the situation?"

Consider the answer then follow up with the next question

"How can I respond now in a way that would make the people I respect and care about be proud of my actions?"

If you can always ask these questions honourably and honestly, then the answers will lead your behaviour away from emotion-led responses towards thoughtful and reasoned reactions.

Finally, consider which action feeds which wolf. Each time you do this, you present yourself the opportunity to feed the right (or the wrong) wolf.

CHAPTER 10

Acta non Verba

"The only thing that is constant is change."
– Heraclitus

Who are you and who do you want to be?

Often, we talk about the person we'd like to be in life, the person we're working towards becoming tomorrow with today's actions; this is our 'Ideal-Self'.

Also, we're confronted by the person we see in the mirror each morning, the person we cannot hide from as it is the reflection we see presented back to us every day; our 'Self-Image'. This can be understood by exploring Carl Rogers' Self Theory.

As humans, we often describe the person we want to be without really taking enough action to become it. We can be guilty of espousing our philosophy of life rather than choosing to embody it: "Acta non verba". Also, the distance between our 'Ideal-Self' (future) and our 'Self-Image' (present) can create incongruency and by its very nature, inhibit our potential to self-actualise the future 'Ideal-Self'.

Consider for a moment if your future 'Ideal-Self' in no way resembled your actual 'Self-Image'. You would either be living a lie and in denial or crippled by low self-esteem, due to the widening gap between your two 'selves'.

The great thing, though, is you can always change and evolve. You're not the same person you were when you started reading this book. Precisely the same way I am not the same person as before I began the process of writing it – this is the eternal reward of self-improvement. As an example, I have noticed a considerable improvement in my conversational vernacular, born and nurtured via the process of researching and writing this book over many months. Every day is an opportunity to evolve our *self*, and reflection and personal development gives rise to this when you commit yourself to the task.

Reflection: When trapped in our fixed 'Self-Image', we sacrifice the ability to grow because we fool ourselves into believing that our 'self' is a fixed entity. We are, in fact, continually changing and evolving, sometimes without realising. Take every opportunity to close the gap between your two 'selves' and watch your 'Self-Esteem' grow due to your commitment and application.

People don't struggle in difficult situations; they struggle when they don't adapt to situations.

CHAPTER 11

Ten Two Letter Words

"To be like the rock which the waves keep crashing over. It stands unmoved as the raging sea falls still around it."
– Marcus Aurelius

I vividly remember my time training to become a Royal Marine Commando. I also remember the point in training I was at my weakest. It was approaching the end of my Commando training in late summer of 1999; the finish line was in sight. For many aspiring Royal Marine Commandos, completing the famous Commando tests represents the ultimate physical and mental test, a 'dark night of the soul' experience. This was not the case for me. I found all four Commando tests enjoyable and had built their significance up so much in my mind that the imagined perception of difficulty far outweighed the actual reality. My 'dark night of the soul' moments would come after the Commando tests during the final exercise of Royal Marine training; aptly called 'Final Ex'.

During this exercise, which I began with a painful and swollen right knee, Commandos in training complete something called the 'Killer Yomp', and for me, it certainly lived up to its namesake! Killer Yomp is around twenty miles of hiking across Dartmoor carrying up to 120lbs in your bergen (rucksack). It felt as though I was carrying the world across my shoulders, both physically and metaphorically. The straps on my bergen had restricted the blood flow, and I felt tingling in my fingers. There was no position to move the straps to that offered meaningful respite from my torture. Each step seemed to contain unimaginable pain and require immeasurable determination. I could not envisage completing the next twenty metres, never mind the next twenty miles. My body ached all over, especially my injured right knee, which felt like it exploded with every step. Although trying to contain my emotion, I could not control the occasional audible outburst of despair, which I knew would yield me no mercy. I was nearly finished in mind and body. But something stopped me quitting that night, and it wasn't the adrenaline-fuelled theme music from Rocky or an inspirational video from YouTube.

It was the 10 x 2 letter words I kept repeating with my internal dialogue: **"If it is to be, it is up to me."** I have always believed that life can be summed up by these simple words. **"If it is to be, it is up to me."**

There are times when superfluous words are needed to raise a person's courage and passion for achieving greatness. Rousing speeches from outstanding orators such as Winston Churchill, Barack Obama or even Adolf Hitler, can raise the hairs on the back of the listener's neck, with good or bad actions to follow. These speeches stir our very emotions, and when delivered with passion and sincerity, can have a tumultuous effect on the human collective.

However, I have made a principle to reduce complexity down to the bare essence of what is needed – those 10 x 2 letter words.

Reflection: This does not mean we don't need support from people around us in our lives; of course we do. We are highly sociable creatures that have always thrived in tribes and groups. In many ways, that is what Royal Marine training is all about. I'm suggesting that ultimately, if you apply these 10 x 2 letter words to nearly all situations, it will arouse action in you, and action leads to change and progress. As I reflect on that torturous final exercise, I knew there was no one else who could carry my bergen. If I wanted to gain my coveted Green Beret, I needed to finish the task at hand. I often consider these powerful ten words that have served me so well throughout the years. The Stoics believed in simplicity, the stripping back of unnecessary complications to reveal the pure essence of truth that lies beneath. This concept is wonderfully brought to life with the above statement. You are both the obstacle and the way around at the same time, and much of life is about getting out of the way of yourself.

CHAPTER 12

The Difference Between Winning & Losing Is Only Inches

"*Time is too slow for those who wait, too swift for those who fear, too long for those who grieve, too short for those who rejoice, but for those who love, time is eternity.*"
– ***Henry Van Dyke***

The inches of victory referred to in the chapter title are not the dip for the line in a race; they are the few inches that reside between your ears. Cultivating a positive mindset is about doing the right things daily and being committed to the task in hand. The Stoics knew that developing their philosophy was not an episodic event like going on holiday once a year. It was a continuous succession of small, sometimes unperceivable actions and behaviours – as frequent and necessary as waking from sleep or eating food.

Everybody should meditate for at least fifteen minutes per day unless you're too busy, then you should do it for thirty minutes.

In truth, and sometimes this is uncomfortable, we can always find time for things we WANT to do, but they're not always the things we SHOULD be doing. The key is investing that time into the habits and activities that will reward us, not wasting this precious commodity on activities that bear no fruit. Consider your use of time as a resource, and how you use this time in certain activities brings you a return on your investment. How much time in every twenty-four hours do you allow to slip away without any return?

For example, spending quality time with your family or friends produces a return on investment measured by the strengthening bond between the family and friends. This is done so by the creation of positive experiences and memories that fortify the relationships' invisible bonds. Investing time in going to the gym produces a health return, enabling you to become stronger and reducing your likelihood of illness while improving your physical and mental wellbeing. Spending time scrolling social media returns very little on your time investment, but we can all be guilty of this misuse of time as a resource – myself included! Deciding to eat some fast food offers us the opportunity to reinvest the time it would have taken to prepare a nutritious meal in another area at the point in time. I can't help but suspect that many who choose this time-saving opportunity pay another health-related price over time that's more difficult to rebalance. There is always consequence to both action and inaction. Time is the ultimate judge of decisions, good and bad.

Reflection: Once you adopt this mindset of scrutinising your time allocation and treating time as it should be treated, like a finite resource, it will allow you to start investing your allocation into activities that bring you the greatest return. It is vital to cultivate small positive behaviours that provide a return on our temporal investment.

1. Audit your daily time usage.
2. Categorise the investments of time that bring you the most reward down to the least reward.
3. Discipline yourself and pay attention to when you're attracted to the 'no reward activities'.
4. Watch your results and productivity grow quickly and exponentially.

Don't spend time, invest it.

CHAPTER 13

Rise & Shine

"On those mornings you struggle with getting up, keep this thought in mind – I am awakening to the work of a human being. Why then am I annoyed that I am going to do what I was made for, the very things for which I was put into this world? Or was I made for this, to cower under the covers and keep warm? It's so pleasurable. Were you then made for pleasure? In short, are you to be cuddled or to exert yourself?"
– Marcus Aurelius

It is always easy to do the easy thing, such is the nature of, well, easy things! Likewise, choosing adversity and opting to take the more challenging road at first glance seems foolish; why would we deliberately choose difficulty and hardship? It should be noted, however, that these two parts are different. There are choices in everything you do. Each morning you face your first choice between the adversity of getting out of bed and the comfort of staying under the warm covers. This first primer decision awaits you the very moment your eyes open: *Do I get up and seize the day or do I 'snooze' the alarm?*

You face your first juncture – comfort or hardship?

Humans will nearly always choose comfort before discomfort when afforded the choice. This is precisely why many of us hit the snooze button, even if it only rewards us fleeting moments under the warmth of our duvets.

I call this first decision of the day 'The Window'.

It is the window of opportunity to achieve your first win of the day and orientate yourself for further successful decisions. Making the wrong decision at the window will usually predict more easy options and perhaps poor judgment errors. When you make the right decision in the window, it encourages you to make another good decision, and good decisions create positive momentum. The more momentum you build up, the harder the train is to stop. This forward momentum can quickly gather positive, or negative, momentum, so this first decision can easily shape your entire day. This day can define your week and a succession of these weeks shape your entire year. You might think I am overdramatising such a simple and seemingly insignificant moment, but you would be wrong to conclude this. How you do something, is how you do everything. Also, in my experience, if you cannot exercise the mindset over small (manageable) decisions, you will most likely not have the resolve to make the right decisions with more significant commitments. Resilience is a learnable skill that is shaped by our seemingly insignificant micro-decisions. You are where you are today primarily as consequence of the cumulative effect of each small decision you've ever made just as I am where I am. We are the inescapable consequence of choice.

Reflection: It took me a considerable amount of time and soul searching to admit these things to myself. I used to pass off my lack of discipline in such areas saying; 'It is just who I am.' It was unchangeable. It was irreversibly part of my individual genetic composition and not within my circle of influence to change this hardwiring of my personality type. I now know this absolutely to be bullshit. Applying the Stoics' principles to my behaviour, I was eventually forced to awkwardly acknowledge that I was just making excuses because I didn't want to change. In all honesty, I liked the comfort of easy options; as I said, easy options are nice *because* they're easy.

Place your focus at the first moment and act with decisiveness and commitment. If you do this, the rest will take care of itself. Choose the reward you want for your decisions. Weakness, excuses and fragility are the reward you will surely reap from easy choices, while resilience, results and fortitude are the reward for choosing adversity.

CHAPTER 14

Stoicism Virtue 2/4 – Justice

"Live out your life in truth and justice, tolerant of those who are neither true nor just."
– ***Marcus Aurelius***

Justice is an interesting concept that cannot be easily defined and should not be confused with the 'laws of the land'. Different cultures have different laws and may have varying interpretations of what 'just' behaviour fits within the framework of these laws. Added to this, different eras undoubtedly espouse contrasting levels of social acceptance, easily observed in the 'cancel culture' and 'virtue signalling' of today, often referred to as the 'snowflake' generation. It is sometimes suggested that we live in 'soft' times. I do not necessarily agree with this over-simplification of complex societal issues, however, I agree that never before have we lived in such a climate of division and separation. The chasm has grown between the left and the right, the haves and the have nots, the religious and the atheists. Justice seems inextricably bound inside a world in which knowing whether the news I consume is 'fake news' or actual events is becoming as challenging as separating which religion represents God's accurate word.

I often wonder what the ancient philosophers of antiquity would have made of the world we now occupy. Is the world more or less 'just' with the passing of 2,000 years?

The Collins dictionary describes justice as "just behaviour or treatment", which in turn leads to "a concern for justice, peace, and genuine respect for people".

Acting in a just way isn't always easy, but having the words of Marcus Aurelius near will undoubtedly help. The final part of his quote resonates most strongly with me: *"tolerant of those who are neither true nor just."* This is perhaps the greatest of all challenges and certainly something I am yet to attain; to forgive those whose behaviour does not deserve forgiveness.

It is often those who disregard our moral standards that trigger the most potent emotional response. It predominately hijacks our natural emotional reactions rather than our thoughtful and logical 'just' thinking. You can observe this by the projection of a person's beliefs on their social media feeds and their subsequent condemnation of opposing views. Political bias is usually a good place to notice such contempt for personal difference. It is always easy to agree with the people who agree with us, or as the saying goes: 'yoghurt likes yoghurt'.

Can you listen to opposing beliefs and remain calm in conversation, or do the opposition's words expose the fragility of your indifference?

The Greek Stoics welcomed the opportunity to test their virtues. Fundamentally, the key to mastering your reactions is to interpret challenging situations as opportunities to place your integrity to the test and strengthen your ability to remain just, even in the company of those that are *"neither true nor just."*

Reflection: A possible place to begin developing this 'just' quality is to examine when you did not exercise reasoned behaviour in the past. Reflect on both your actions and reactions and, whenever possible, atone for this by correcting the injustice that may have incurred. A simple apology may quickly remedy this. Few people like admitting their wrongdoings or misjudgements. Perhaps the thought of this will encourage you to choose a 'just' reaction to any situation rather than apologise in the wake of ill-judgement.

CHAPTER 15

Want Nothing = Have Everything

"No person has the power to have everything they want, but it is in their power not to want what they don't have, and to cheerfully put to use what they do have."
– Seneca

One of our Western 'capitalist' culture's most incredible tricks is to trap us on the hamster wheel of 'desire'. In many ways, we've been conned into thinking that happiness sits on the other side of success, and success can be measured by "the acquisition and public display of the things that we desire in life", as Seneca pointed out.

The problem with this is the endlessness bound within it, and there is always more to have.

You achieve good grades; you want to get better ones. You get the promotion at work you've worked towards for two years; very quickly you normalise this new reality and set your sights on the next promotion. You have a nice car; you want a better one. You have a three-bedroom house; you want a four-bedroom house with a more extensive lawn (which you'll most likely resent cutting).

Think about how happy you would have been five years ago with the things you have now, but then also consider what you have today that you desired so strongly last year. Promotion, salary, phone, car, house and holidays can always be 'improved' in the future. Our unquenchable desire for these material possessions can rob us of our ability to be grateful for the non-material possessions of life. It forces our focus of attention towards the 'cognitive horizon', or as Professor Shawn Achor from Harvard University eloquently observes, "If we work hard, we can be successful, and only when we're successful can we then be happy."

There is a massive flaw in this life philosophy, insomuch as it places happiness beyond an undefined point in the future and behind achievements and possessions which we are yet to attain. When doing this, we demote the beauty of the journey by fixating on the destination. Most likely, you have been guilty, as I have, of delaying and postponing happiness and contentedness until you have achieved the material goals in life. If we were to stop for a moment, we might recognise the absurdity of this obsessional pursuit, and perhaps the impermanence of the material prize.

Maybe there is no more remarkable example of this than our obsession with phone upgrades. Your current phone can most likely do everything you could ever ask from a phone. Why do many of us upgrade at the first opportunity once the newer, fancier, shiny, more desirable phone is released? It seems as though our magpie gene is collectively caught on this bi-annual rollercoaster. Experiencing the initial high of unwrapping the new, upgraded and ever so sexily packaged phone, before the gentle decline, as the initial obsession evaporates and it becomes just a 'phone', before finally rising again towards the inevitable future upgrade. Perhaps many of us are hypnotised by the social proofing and identity of owning the newest, best (est), fanciest phone available – whether we need it or not. As uncomfortable as it is, many of us are on this commercial hamster wheel.

Reflection: Being Stoic was not about rejecting the nice things in life; Seneca was very wealthy indeed. However, it does call for reasoned thinking, temperance, and self-awareness. Never before have we had such access to the things we desire. Take time to reflect on unreasonable desires as opposed to reasonable wants as this is very much worthy of all of our considerations. A £30 watch and a £3,000 watch both tell the same time and both are equally accurate at predicting your death.

"How much time he saves who does not look to see what his neighbour says or does or thinks."

– Marcus Aurelius

CHAPTER 16

What Kind of Boxer are You?

"But what is philosophy? Doesn't it simply mean preparing ourselves for what may come? Don't you understand that really amounts to saying that if I would so prepare myself to endure, then let anything happen that will? Otherwise, it would be like the boxer exiting the ring because he took some punches. Actually, you can leave the boxing ring without consequence, but what advantage would come from abandoning the pursuit of wisdom? So, what would each of us say to every trial we face? This is what I've trained for, this is my discipline!"

– Epictetus

Many people consider Mike Tyson one of the modern greats of boxing. In many ways he is, in other ways perhaps it's more questionable. Maybe it is this very paradox that makes him such a fascinating and divisive character?

Tyson was undoubtedly a supremely talented boxer who should have dominated the heavyweight class for many more years than he did. Ill-discipline led to his eventual downfall, both inside the ring and out. He was finally reduced to biting Evander Holyfield's ear at the end of his downward spiralling career. One of the elements I find fascinating about Tyson's legacy is when he was met with adversity, and how he reacted to the adversity presented to him. As a young fighter Tyson would dominate fighters from the outset, setting a blistering pace in the early rounds. Because of his brutal onslaught, Tyson was rarely fighting under pressure or on the back foot. Added to this, he projected an aura of invincibility that undoubtedly weighed heavily on the minds of his adversaries.

Buster Douglas would be the first fighter to go past this air of invincibility, and when tested severely, Tyson's aura disappeared.

Going into the Buster Douglas fight on February 11th, 1990, Mike Tyson was 37-0 with thirty-three knockouts. Douglas was the considerable underdog at odds of 42:1 with most bookmakers. Perhaps Douglas fought the fight of his life, and maybe Tyson was slightly below par? Regardless, Buster Douglas fought superbly, and when he knocked Tyson out in the 10th round, he created one of boxing's greatest upsets and memorable nights. Tyson went on to rebuild his career with seven straight wins. He regained two of his belts before Evander Holyfield famously deposed him in their epic first fight, aptly named 'Finally' because of the length of time it had taken for the two heavyweights to meet each other professionally.

It is only in times of adversity that we can genuinely measure greatness, and when we cannot rise to that adversity, we suddenly become mortal; no matter how immortal we once appeared.

Reflection: Life can be a boxing match at times, sometimes it can leave you bloodied on the canvas, occasionally even knocked out for the count, but as with all great boxers it is the heart to carry on that shapes your results. It is in the fire of adversity that the potential for growth and the forging of resilience resides. Without doubt, there are many lessons that can be drawn from the philosophy of boxing.

As the great Rocky Balboa said, *"It's not how hard you hit that counts, it's how hard you can get hit and keep going."*

CHAPTER 17

Stoic Principle – Recognise There Is Life After Failure

"Does what's happened keep you from acting with justice, generosity, self-control, sanity, prudence, honesty, humility, straightforwardness, and all other qualities that allow a person's nature to fulfill itself? So remember this principle when something threatens to cause you pain: the thing itself was no misfortune at all; to endure it and prevail is great good fortune."

– Marcus Aurelius, Meditations

The Story of Rocky

In the early 1970s Sylvester Stallone was a struggling actor in Hollywood. Money was becoming so tight that he had to choose between having enough money for food or keeping his dog. He sold his dog with a heavy heart as he feared he could not even feed him properly. One evening he had the opportunity to watch the Muhammad Ali versus Chuck

Wepner fight. Wepner was a complete unknown fighting against possibly the greatest boxer ever to live. On that night Wepner would give his all in the ring and even knocked the champion down at one point. Stallone watched in awe and immediately saw the metaphor for his life. He left the fight and wrote the script for Rocky in three days straight in his apartment.

Stallone took the script to producers around Hollywood and most turned it down flat. Some showed interest, but nothing seemed to go past that stage. That was until he auditioned for another part but, as with most of his auditions, he was unsuccessful. Before leaving though he took a chance and offered his script to the director. The director read the script and loved it. Chartoff-Winkler Productions offered Stallone $360,000 for the script, however, there was one problem: they did not want Stallone to act in his film. Stallone, even though he was utterly broke, turned the offer down.

Stallone later said, "I thought, 'You know what? You've got this poverty thing down. You don't need much to live on.' I sort of figured it out. I was in no way used to the good life. So, I knew in the back of my mind that if I sell this script and it does very well, I'm going to jump off a building if I'm not in it. There's no doubt in my mind. I'm going to be very, very upset. So, this is one of those things, when you just roll the dice and fly by the proverbial seat of your pants, and you just say, 'I've got to try it. I've just got to do it. I may be totally wrong, and I'm going to take a lot of people down with me, but I just believe in it.'"

Eventually, the producers relented and agreed to pay Stallone $1 million, which made it a relatively low-budget film, even in the 1970s. To make the film within budget Stallone used family members in the production team and many of the scenes were shot first time to ensure the film did not run over budget. Stallone even shot many of the scenes on handheld cameras to conserve the budget further.

Even at the premiere, it was uncertain whether the film would bomb, but after the first screening momentum grew and grew. Rocky was nominated for nine academy awards and took home three. It is estimated to have grossed over $200 million with the entire Rocky movie franchise earning over $1.4 billion!

Reflection: There will always be setbacks in life; of this, you can be confident. Some of these setbacks can, at times, seem insurmountable and the temptation to quit overwhelming. No matter how much it might feel like you're failing you only really yield when you give up. The winners in life are usually the ones who persevered ten minutes longer than everyone else. That's what defines them; their disregard for throwing the towel in, even when forced to sell their dog!

CHAPTER 18

Carpe Diem

"Let us therefore set out wholeheartedly, leaving aside our many distractions and exert ourselves in this single purpose, before we realise too late the swift and unstoppable flight of time and are left behind. As day arises, welcome it as the very best day of all, and make it your own possession. We must seize what flees."

– Seneca

My fiancée (perhaps wife by the time this book is published) Ruth has cancer, or leukaemia to be precise, or to be even more precise chronic myeloid leukaemia (CML). There is currently no cure for CML, but it is managed successfully with oral chemotherapy taken twice daily, every day without fail. Like a metronome, every twelve hours, for the rest of her life.

She has the words 'Carpe Diem' tattooed on her right ankle, which we had inked in Athens over my 40th birthday in

2018. The accurate translation being 'pluck the fruit whilst it's ripe' or more commonly known as 'seize the day'. The meaning of this to her is that each day is a gift, and often we wait until we stare death in the face before we appreciate what it truly means to be alive. In essence, we all have a choice – we can let the day take us with familiarity and comfort, or we can seize it, like grasping hard the base of the nettle plant knowing that to act cautiously will usually result in pain. But to work with commitment and decisiveness will prevent the nettle stinging.

Occasionally we chat about the time in her life when she was first diagnosed and extremely ill, which was before we knew each other. It's fascinating as a performance coach to comprehend the mindset required to endure the immense suffering she did, from lumber puncture needles in the base of her spine, to weight and hair loss, without mentioning the rapid erosion of her dignity through relentless physical examinations. In our conversations, she describes her private despair at the realisation she might not live to see her 21st birthday. In these dark moments, her regrets were not of the 'things' she didn't have – the new phone or expensive shoes were not the things she desired during this 'dark night of the soul'. She yearned for the things she had not yet experienced, as opposed to the things she had not yet possessed. The places she had yet to visit, the food she had not been able to taste, the cultures which were still unknown to her, and the experiences of life that were at that point unfulfilled.

If you examine and audit your life, the memories that most likely come to your awareness are not when you bought something new, or the unboxing of your new Apple phone or laptop. Lovely as these things indeed are, they only ever provide temporary satisfaction. Your memories will most likely be of experiences you had, with people you care about, that define special periods in your life.

Reflection: Every day should be grasped like a nettle without flinching and with disregard to what *might* go wrong. Focus on all the positives that *could* happen with each day. Reflect now to when the last time you indeed seized the day by the scruff of the neck. When your time arrives, will you stare death in the face and wonder about all of the days lost in the bed of comfort, or will you smile wryly at the life well lived? Make today count.

CHAPTER 19

There Is Nothing Wrong With Being Wrong

"If anyone can prove and show me that I think and act in error I will gladly change it – for I seek the truth by which no one has ever been harmed. The one who is harmed is the one who abides in deceit and ignorance."
– Marcus Aurelius

For centuries humans have been cursed by dogmatic thinking, unable to progress because of a combination of stubbornness, pride, and arrogance or – as it's otherwise known – 'hubris'. Do not ever be concerned with, or afraid of, being wrong; only be worried about and afraid of being proven wrong without the humility, flexibility, and emotional intelligence to adjust your position.

The late, great Stephen Hawking was famously quoted as saying, *"Intelligence is the ability to adapt to change."*

As we first explored in Chapter 14 the Greek Stoics focused on being 'just' instead of the futile attempt in subjectively judging right and wrong. Today's right can often become tomorrow's wrong, and today's wrong sometimes matures into tomorrow's right. All we can ever hope for is to remain humble and open-minded to the ever-changing reality we occupy, knowing that our certainties and sureties will occasionally not stand the test of time.

An excellent example of this is the Aristotelian theory that our earth is the known universe's centre. The Catholic Church embraced Aristotle's ideas primarily because they loosely aligned with scripture and supported the Church's beliefs. It took over 1,500 years and the incredible bravery of a handful of scientists and astrologists to disprove this long-held belief. Specifically, Galileo Galilei, Nicolaus Copernicus and Johannes Kepler, who all contributed to the concept of the 'Helio Centric' model in which Earth, and the other planets, orbited the sun – not that the sun orbited the earth.

Consider how many positions of 'certainty' you have taken in dispute, only to be later illuminated by the very inconsistencies within that position.

The most famous philosopher for exercising this in debate was the great Socrates. Using his 'dialectical' method of questioning, he would ask his adversary questions to determine their position's basic principles in the debate. More often than not, the person's own logic would disprove their erroneous claims, leading Socrates to be known as 'the gadfly of Athens'.

Reflection: Being right and being wrong can change quickly, so attach little value to either perspective. Instead, look to behave in a 'just' and honourable way, always reserving enough humility to change your mind when presented with new information. Today, it seems that there has never been such abundance of information in our species' history, while paradoxically wisdom, critical thinking, and knowledge seem to be in opposing decline.

Perhaps part of the appeal for books such as this one, that retrospectively look for the wisdom to move forward, centres around the flexibility and acceptance that we're all condemned to be gloriously wrong from time-to-time!

CHAPTER 20

The Truth about Progress

"We are what we repeatedly do. Excellence, then, is not an act, but a habit."
– Aristotle

We are but a mere sack of skin supported by an internal scaffold-type structure comprising bones, cartilage and ligament, and psychologically bound together cohesively by our daily habits and quirks of personality. Or in the words of Richard Dawkins, we are but "*gigantic lumbering robots*".

Have you ever considered how much of your life is programmed and executed repeatedly, and often away from your awareness? In many ways, your goal in life shouldn't be about eradicating bad habits, rather the pursuit of nurturing and cultivating positive ones that bring reward. Habits are indeed such a peculiar 'ism' of the human race.

Imagine for a moment there is an ice cube on the table in front of you, and the room is 26°F in temperature. You would be able to see your breath in front of you, and you would most likely need gloves and coat as the room would be uncomfortably cold otherwise. The ice cube, at this temperature, would remain unchanged. If you increased the temperature by one degree to 27°, the ice cube would stay intact, and the difference would be imperceptible by your senses. Once again, if you increased the temperature by another one degree to 28°, you would experience the same result. At 29° the ice cube would remain unchanged and the increase would be barely noticeable. Increasing the temperature to 30°, then 31°, would still effect no change. However, once you reached 32°F, the ice cube would begin melting, and with each degree after that, the rate of change would increase rapidly.

Ask yourself, what was the pivotal degree of temperature change? You might be mistaken in presuming that the shift from 31° to 32° was the most important, although the temperature reflected the change in circumstance. In truth, each incremental rise of 1° was equally crucial to the one that came before and the one that followed. One of our species' many curious traits is we tend only to notice something when we become conscious of it. Otherwise, it conceals itself from our awareness.

Habits are like this. You won't often see the fruits of our labour early on, barely noticing either positive or negative changes, but should you persist there is always a critical point when observable change occurs. The key to understanding this is to know that each hidden incremental change is as significant as the visible changes that occur, usually at the end.

How many gold prospectors have abandoned their pursuit only a few strikes away from their dream?

Reflection: Developing conscious awareness of your habits is the first step to shaping and changing if necessary. Once you have become aware of the pattern, the next stage is to understand the triggers that initiate it; is it the people you're with, the environment you're in, or a specific contextualised scenario? Once you know this, you have the opportunity to work towards eradicating the habits that are not serving you and start cultivating the positive habits you desire. Too many people are enslaved by their habits and resign themselves to a fate they need not. Habits can be changed when applying some of the virtues and principles of Stoicism. Anything that the mind can create can be changed with the correct commitment and application.

CHAPTER 21

Sometimes, Knowledge is the Most Valuable Commodity

"It is greed to do all the talking but not want to listen at all."
– Democritus

In the middle of the industrial revolution, there was once a fable of a man who owned a textile mill just outside Birmingham. The mill owner was greedy and ill-tempered with an appetite for only furthering himself and his interests. He worked hard and demanded his employees do the same. One day, the usual cacophony that bellowed from the mill from morning to night fell silent. The machines that usually banged, whistled, rattled and popped fell completely quiet. On hearing the silence, the mill owner stormed from his office to find out why production had ceased. None of his employees could explain why the engine room had stopped working.

Immediately, he sent his engineers into the steam room to fix the issue, but they could not work out why the machines were silent. The mill owner then sent for an outside company to remedy the problem, but likewise, they too could not understand the reason for the silence. Finally, the mill owner demanded that the most expensive and reputable company in the land be sent for, and regardless of cost, they were to assign their best engineers to the job. They duly arrived and worked for two days and two nights without success. The mill owner had now become distraught with worry. Stress consumed him as he contemplated the spiralling costs of being unable to fix his now silent mill as each day represented lost profits. At this point, there was a gentle tap on the mill owner's office door. The impatient mill owner commanded the person to enter with his usual ill-tempered tone of voice. Into the office strolled a young boy, with only a small bag, walking calmly toward the mill owner's desk. The young boy had heard about the mill owner's plight and had come to offer his assistance in resolving the matter in hand. The mill owner was immediately dismissive of the boy's ability to assist but accepted begrudgingly as he had few options remaining.

The young boy went down into the boiler room and sat on a stool for five minutes listening and observing, before spending a further two minutes walking up and down listening intently. He then took out of his bag a small hammer and started to gently tap at certain bends in the pipework, always listening conscientiously and paying attention to all of his senses. Suddenly, he noticed a slightly different sound with one of his gentle taps. Calmly he walked over, placed the small hammer in the bag and took out his larger hammer. He struck the pipework accurately and cleanly with a swift and decisive blow. Immediately, the machinery burst into life and started whistling, banging, rattling and popping. The noises grew and replaced the silence that had come before. On hearing the noise from the factory floor, the mill owner hastened himself into the engine room with a combination of outright joy and abject relief. He exclaimed to the young boy, "Whatever you were planning to charge me for your services, double it!"

The young boy casually replied, "I will bill you for my time as I originally intended and no more, good sir." When the invoice arrived on the mill owner's desk, he opened it and gasped and choked before quickly boiling with a mixture of rage and disbelief. The invoice appeared to ask for £100, which was twice as much as the most expensive company who had worked for two entire days, and the young boy had only spent ten minutes at work! The mill owner demanded a complete breakdown from the boy explaining how his invoice was so much more than the most expensive company. The boy responded with a new invoice explaining the charges:

> 10 minutes tapping = £1
> Knowing where to tap = £99
> Total = £100

Reflection: I consider myself extremely fortunate to mentor many other coaches. During my mentoring sessions we talk extensively about value and how to effectively price for their services, a topic often sensitive to coaches in my experience. I nearly always tell this story and ask them to consider placing the value on the knowledge they have developed as well as the outcome of their services, as opposed to an hourly rate. Value is so often measured in process where it should really be measured in outcome.

CHAPTER 22

Wealth is Free

"Freedom isn't secured by filling up on your heart's desire but by removing desire from your heart."
– ***Epictetus***

Building on the concept of chapter 15 there are two very different approaches to wealth accumulation. You can either chase the things you desire or desire the things you have. I have long believed that many of the woes of modern humans lay within our obsession with comparison. Social status can sometimes be defined by the 'things' we collect as humans. The pursuit of our personal museum of things indicates our placement within the social hierarchy either above or below the 'Jones'. As technology has evolved, our capacity for comparison has multiplied at a nauseating pace. In the 1980s people were seduced by television advertising to keep up with next doors' 'museum of things'. Children in 2021 are no longer keeping up with the 'Jones'; they're trying to keep up with the Kardashians via a warped and distorted Instagram prism of reality!

These present undeniable dangers for our children, and even more so for the children of our children. The social gap between the haves and have nots has artificially closed, fuelled by the consumer credit explosion. The 'buy now, pay later' mindset creates a false narrative of abundance but beneath the surface lays the private bondage of debt. Young people forever condemned to steal from Peter to pay Paul. We have to find a new way for our children to measure worth and I believe this starts with re-addressing how much we give our children for Christmas and birthdays.

It would be remiss of me not to acknowledge the other comparison traps created by social media through the pursuit of documenting our otherwise ordinary day-to-day life, through the extraordinary filters of social media platforms. The Stoics understood the pitfalls of excess desire and unnecessary comparison 2,300 years ago. However, it would appear over time that these lessons have been forgotten by the endless bombardment of advertising on our senses leading to collective amnesia. We now live in an artificial world, where moments are hyperinflated and captured with filters to present the illusion of perfection and measured with likes and comments. We seldom seem to appreciate these moments in reality as much as we do the acclaim and recognition they bring digitally.

The consequence of this break-neck pursuit of perfectly captured moments is a continuous desire to create the perfect social media moment - to sacrifice the actual moment in time. We are hurtling without purpose towards the next possible opportunity, and in doing so, we allow each present moment to slip away criminally unappreciated. Nothing sharpens our awareness of the present moment more than adversity or tragedy. When we're placed outside of our comfort zone, we suddenly lose our obsession with the future. The past also evaporates from our awareness as our consciousness is sharpened and focused directly on the now. Unfortunately, it often takes adversity or tragedy to focus the lens, but it doesn't have to be this way with conscious living. How much of your day is occupied by where (or when) you need to be next? How much of your day do you document for social media?

Reflection: The main reason I embrace cold water is to strengthen my mind and body but even more importantly, it focuses me intently into the now and reminds me of these precious present moments. What will your thoughts be consumed by when entering the cold water? Will your mind be distracted and think of your next appointment, or will you be consumed by that moment alone? Nature is a razor to the immediacy of life and can bring your mind sharply into focus. My challenge for you is to start having a cold shower each day, but I'll explain more in the next chapter.

CHAPTER 23

Make Friends with the Cold

"We are so successful at being comfortable that comfort has become the enemy of our success."
– *Wim Hof*

In 2016 I found myself with mild burnout after completing a reasonably gruelling sixteen consecutive days teaching at our NLP academy, which at the time was based in Lilleshall, Shropshire. Ironically, and uncomfortably, preventing burnout is a topic I often teach to clients as well as an area of coaching I specialise in. While recovering from my mild burnout (and embarrassment), I decided to embark on some research on my laptop. Specifically, I explored burnout, the nervous system and preventative interventions, primarily to understand how on earth I had found myself in this awkward position. Somehow this search arrived at an eccentric Dutch man called Wim Hof. Wim was relatively unknown at the time, although he was undoubtedly starting to gather momentum online, primarily because of the numerous absurd world records he held. These record attempts, which featured mostly extreme cold and occasionally extreme heat, started attracting mainstream media attention. My curiosity was especially spiked because many of the record attempts were observed and measured objectively by scientists. Wim held records for being submerged up to his neck in ice, swimming the farthest distance underneath the ice, climbing mountains wearing only shorts, and running marathons barefoot in both extreme heat and freezing climates. What he was doing seemed impossible to me.

I started watching all of the material I could find on the internet about Wim and reading any books I could find written by or about him. What amazed me more than anything was the beautiful simplicity of his technique that was broken into three parts:

1. Gradual, non-forced exposure to cold water.
2. Breathwork – Wim developed his technique, which he freely admits is taken from older sources.
3. Mindset – the commitment to go past your perceived limitations and beliefs, and find you are much stronger than you think.

I was hooked! Using only free resources, reading books, and using Wim's app, I found I could not only cope but also be *comfortable* in extreme cold, which is something I had previously thought impossible. The starting point for this exploration of the cold was simply turning my shower from hot to cold!

Reflection: For the next 30 days, I would like you to commit to turning your shower cold at the end of your usual warm shower.

- For the first week aim for 30 seconds of cold at the end of your shower. ***(Breathe calmly)***
- For week two increase this to 1 minute at the end of the shower. ***(Breathe calmly)***
- For week three increase this to 1 minute 30 seconds at the end of the shower. ***(Breathe calmly)***
- For week four increase this to 2 minutes at the end of the shower. ***(Breathe calmly)***

It will be uncomfortable to begin with, and every piece of your internal dialogue will try and talk you out of the experience. This is the basis of this book though – the commitment to taking action which brings positive reward from the adversity. Focus your mind and calm your breathing, slowly in and slowly out. When you pass fifteen days (or even before), you'll notice that what was once incredibly challenging is becoming relatively comfortable. You will be mentally and physically stronger as a result.

CHAPTER 24

Knowledge is Knowing, Wisdom is Knowing You Don't Know Anything

---

"The only true wisdom is in knowing you know nothing."
– Socrates

The Delphic Oracle famously pronounced Socrates as the wisest man in all of Athens. At first, Socrates refused this proclamation because the only thing he was truly confident of was his own ignorance. In his wisdom, Socrates decided to test this prophecy by engaging in dialect with all the other 'wise' men of Athens. In ancient Greece, wise men who taught (for money) were known as 'Sophists'; this is the origin of words such as 'sophisticated'. The etymology of this term originates from the Greek word 'Sophos', meaning wise. Plato would later seek to separate the 'Sophist' from the 'Philosopher' in his treaty, *Sophist*. Plato's conclusion was the Sophists were nothing more than mercenary intellects that profited from the gift of knowledge.

After consulting the Athenian Sophists, Socrates' conclusion was that the Delphic Oracle was in fact correct. He concluded that all the other wise men thought they knew something but knew nothing; Socrates was the only one wise enough to know he knew nothing.

Thomas Edison once famously declared, *"We don't know one millionth of 1% about anything."* And if the inventor of the lightbulb and DC electricity knew this little, imagine how little we know collectively. One thing I think most people can be reasonably certain of is that if both Socrates and Edison were in agreement about the oceans of knowledge they were yet to acquire, then the same can apply to us. Do not allow your mind to become lazy, because laziness will foster an apathetic attitude towards your continued personal growth and development. I urge you emphatically to pursue knowledge and commit yourself to the following philosophy:

"Learn as if you were to live forever, live as if you were to die tomorrow." ***Mahatma Gandhi***

Reflection: Commit to learning every day to maintain your mind's growth and development, regardless of age. The mind should be treated like a muscle and worked out vigorously to its limit of ability, and as frequently as possible.

Try this activity to draw what you don't know from your mind into your awareness. Take a blank piece of paper and write down as many things as you can that you don't know, do this as quickly as possible to encourage speed of thought. Aim for as many as possible, and just keep writing as fast as possible without overthinking. The topics can be anything from history, science, nature, astrology, mathematics, etc. Once you have your list make it your task for the following week to seek understanding in all areas.

Examples:

1. How do they measure the distance to stars?
2. How do bumblebees fly?
3. How did life form on Earth?
4. What was the suffragette movement?
5. What is the longest standing world record in track and field?
6. How and when did the dinosaurs wipe out?
7. Who discovered the planets of our solar system?
8. What does $e=mc^2$ mean?
9. What can I learn in Latin?
10. How does gravity work?
11. How does gravity affect time?
12. How fast is the speed of light?

CHAPTER 25

A Rising Tide Raises All Ships

"Let us also produce some bold act of our own and join the ranks of the most emulated."
– Seneca

The Manchester United football team of the late 1990s were an incredible team who never knew when they were beaten. Renowned for staging late comebacks, such as the two goals that brought them the European Cup in 1999 and overturning the two goal deficit during the semi-final away to Juventus in the previous round. There are many well-documented reasons for this, but most notably they had players who would take the initiative and seize the game, which blended with a team that collectively believed that they could always score, no matter the situation. After Manchester United had won the European Cup in 1999, Roy Keane observed that this quality began to diminish, and a few years later they surrendered the Premiership to Arsenal.

Unlike previous seasons, the players began waiting for each other to seize the moment and drive forward to snatch victory from the jaws of defeat. They had lost their capacity to rescue victory from the jaws of defeat. In life, you can be the ascending surge that raises all the ships, or the descending tide which drops them, or even the vessels themselves, passive and submissive to both the rise and fall around you. When you take the initiative and seize the moment, you raise those around you and inspire others into action. The catalyst for change can be found in the slightest spark and subsequently creates the most ferocious fire. It's not always easy to be the person who seizes the moment and shapes the culture of those around. It takes courage, determination and commitment to act decisively in such situations.

The world has more than enough vessels being risen and lowered passively, and we need more tidal forces rising in these uncertain times. An excellent example is the Swedish schoolgirl turn environmentalist, Greta Thunberg. Regardless of whether you agree with her environmental views or not, you cannot disagree with her effect on mobilising the collective voices of millions of humans around the world. Her singular action of refusing to go to school so she could silently protest outside the Swedish government buildings each Friday in 2015 slowly gathered momentum. It struck an emotional chord with young people around the world. Within a few years, and supported by #FridaysforFuture on social media, up to 20,000 students were also striking. The purpose of these strikes was to hold governments accountable to meet the carbon emissions targets set during the Paris agreement in 2015.

One young girl, aged fifteen, managed to create a movement that sent waves around the world and unified the voice of young people in all corners of the globe.

As Barack Obama famously said, *"One voice can change a room, and if one voice can change a room, then it can change a city, and if it can change a city, it can change a state, and if it can change a state, it can change a nation, and if it can change a nation, it can change the world. Your voice can change the world."*

Reflection: I have often had the privilege of knowing such people, and I hope that at times I have been that person myself, albeit not as frequently as I would like. We all have the innate ability to be the spark that turns the tide and initiates the rising of the vessels around. Be that voice when the opportunity presents itself.

Be the rising tide for the vessels around you.

NB. The original interpretation of this metaphor is often used to illustrate the connectiveness between ships rising and falling in accordance with the tide. We have deviated slightly from this path by becoming the tide itself in a metaphorical sense.

CHAPTER 26

Funny How That Works Out

"As for me, I would choose being sick over living in luxury, for being sick only harms the body, whereas luxury destroys both the body and soul."
– Musonius Rufus

When was the last time you stopped to appreciate the small things in life? Can you recall the last time you took a breath and felt overwhelmingly grateful as if it was your last? When was the last time you appreciated merely being alive? Able to observe the colours, smells, tastes, sounds and sensations of life itself?

In truth, few do this consistently, if ever at all. Sometimes, we are passengers riding through life with the misperception that we hold the steering wheel in our hands. Moments pass us by like a river takes a stick away towards the sea.

The ancient Greek philosopher Parmenides believed that it was futile to pursue what reality was because it didn't exist.

Instead, he thought that reality was just a grand illusion projected onto humans' minds to occupy them through the mundanity of existence. I'm not so certain about this claim personally, alluring as it most certainly is. Still, if we are entertaining a Matrix-type illusion described by Parmenides, I would prefer to make the most of the experience, however illusory it may be. If we assume that Parmenides (and for that matter Elon Musk) is correct, then this presents us the opportunity to bend and shape our reality to our benefit. Obviously in the spirit of 'it's not real so we may as well enjoy every moment'!

Now, should they both be wildly wrong with their metaphysics (and the matter I feel beneath my fingers in the form of a MacBook as I type is real), this leads us in a different direction. Enjoy every moment because at some undesignated point in time, the music will stop for us all, and we shall have to face the 'reality' of our mortality. Either way, enjoy the ride!

There are many stories about lottery winners who share a common experience. A common experience is that they were often happier before winning their money than they were after. Sometimes they lose friends, family, marriages, and describe their lives turning into living nightmares riddled with mistrust and suspicion. Alternatively, cancer survivors, after going through the very thing most of us fear most – the impending realisation of our mortality – often describe this 'dark night of the soul' experience as the most defining lesson of their life and feel a paradigm shift in their view of what true happiness and contentedness are.

Reflection: No amount of luxury separates the fact that we are all human, born into this world with nothing and destined to leave with the same. As previously explored in chapter 15, will your life be measured by the pursuit of material possessions or immaterial memories and experiences? At the final curtain call will you rue things you hadn't bought, or the experiences you didn't seize?

Funny how that works out, isn't it?

CHAPTER 27

You're a Genius

"Everyone is a genius. But if you judge a fish by its ability to climb a tree, it will live its whole life believing it is stupid."
– Albert Einstein

There is a wonderful book called *How to Think Like Leonardo Da Vinci* by Michael J. Gelb. The book is centred around the eight distinct types of intelligence humans possess; Da Vinci was one of the few people in history to possess all of these different intelligences at genius level:

- Linguistic
- Bodily-Kinaesthetic
- Intra-personal
- Interpersonal
- Naturalist
- Spatial
- Logical-Reasoning
- Musical

Often in life, and specifically in modern culture, we only recognise a few of these as a true intelligence, which is why Western schooling systems are organised to appreciate some more so than others. In truth, the pursuit of them all is a worthy cause, and identifying elements in which you aren't as naturally gifted will undoubtedly bring you the most significant rewards. Frequently, people who perceive themselves as 'not musical' will rarely pick up an instrument – even if the thought of playing the instrument excites their mind and stirs them to the core. We tend to put ourselves in boxes according to our perceived ability and focus all energy and attention into developing the things we're already 'good' at. This is, of course, understandable and very much a human trait. Few people practice painting with their feet because the results are so much worse than with their hands. When hands are no longer an option, adapting with feet becomes necessary, often with quite breath-taking results.

I know this because of my own self-limiting beliefs surrounding my intelligence, learning capabilities and capacity. I have also often heard my clients recount very similar stories they've been telling themselves for years:

"I can't recall a word I read, so don't bother reading books anymore."

"I tried learning a new language, but I gave up after a month or so because it wasn't going in."

"I have always wanted to paint / dance / play guitar / give a presentation / complete an Ironman... but I just know I'd be useless at it."

The truth is, the ability to do all of these things is absolutely within the capabilities of us all, it's just easier to tell ourselves we *can't* do something rather than facing the pressure of actually having to turn up and do it!

Reflection: There is so much to be gained from trying what we perhaps don't naturally get drawn to, or possibly believe we cannot do. Making new synaptic connections and improving your brain in several different areas should never be judged a poor use of time. You might not think the results are worthy of your eyes or ears, but your brain will undoubtedly enjoy the cognitive workout nonetheless. Consider this, your favourite artist once couldn't paint, your favourite musician was hopeless at some point, and your favourite chef with multiple Michelin stars, once couldn't cook. Step out of your limiting box from time-to-time, and you might find hidden potential!

CHAPTER 28

Gnothi Seauton

"Man know thyself; then thou shalt know the Universe and God."
– Pythagoras

One of my coaching mottos is 'Gnothi Seauton' (Greek), which means 'Know Thyself'.

Know Thyself was a common phrase used by Socrates when teaching in the ancient agora in Athens. However, it has also been attributed to much earlier philosophers such as Thales of Miletus and Pythagoras, as well as scribed as a Delphic maxim. Some of Socrates' philosophical ideas were absorbed by Zeno of Citium to eventually create Stoicism. Part of my coaching methodology uses constant self-reflection or practising the art of 'Knowing Thyself'. It is our exploration and subsequent understanding of the world inside that leads to the mastery of the world outside.

You cannot hope for peace outside before mastering harmony inside.

There have been countless examples throughout modern human history of people mastering the world outside (material) without ever achieving mastery of their inner world (nonmaterial). Conquest of the external world can lead to material wealth, success, and an abundance of possessions, but these things rarely return happiness for the person without internal peace.

The burning question that remains is how do we achieve the internal wealth of happiness and peace inside to complement the reality outside?

One of the purposes of facing adversity is to understand yourself better. Human evolution is inextricably tied to the expansion of limiting beliefs about ourselves; both individually and collectively. As described in earlier chapters, for me, cold water and nature provide some of the most authentic teachers of adversity, and the lessons I have learned from embracing cold water have been profound.

I have always feared the cold and have avoided being cold whenever and wherever possible for most of my adult life. When I was twenty years old, I completed Royal Marine Commandos training at (CTCRM) Lympstone, Devon. Throughout the eleven months I spent at Lympstone the thing I feared most was cold and believe me, I became familiar with the feeling of being cold. Above all, it was the constant dread of it happening at any point in time without my concession. Learning to overcome this fear of the cold, and eventually embracing it as a friend, not an enemy, was a profound shift in my mentality which allowed me to experience an inner strength previously unknown.

Most people would believe they could not swim in the Baltic Sea in Northern Sweden in January. They absolutely can but *choose* not to through what I call the 'comfort addiction' that blights modern humans.

We're capable of so much more than we think. It's the limits of our minds that create our limiting beliefs and the only way to test these limitations is by being at the edge of what you perceive possible. To honestly *'Know Thyself'* you have to explore the hidden potential behind your curtain of comfort.

Reflection: Have you started the cold showers from Chapter 23? If not, why not – what's preventing you? If you are, how are you finding this challenge? Are you beginning to realise your inner strength? Are you getting to *'Know Thyself'* yet?

Step into the dark to reveal the light, this alone is the path to knowing yourself.

CHAPTER 29

Irritated Oysters Make Pearls

"That which does not kill us makes us stronger."
– Friedrich Nietzsche

Few people realise this famous quote, often used conversationally to understand hardship, comes from the great modern philosopher Friedrich Nietzsche. Like many great philosophical quotes, it is simple yet eloquently powerful with incredible depth. At the same time, perhaps its true meaning has been lost through subjective interpretation, translation, dilution and repetition? Nietzsche referred to the ongoing perpetual struggle of man, and how that very struggle shaped and defined our existence while determining our future. It is in the same struggle and hardship we discover our purpose, for, without pain, we can never truly know pleasure. Likewise, to use some of Georg Wilhelm Hegel's philosophical method.

"If our pain is the thesis and the antithesis is pleasure, then the synthesis is undoubtedly the bridge of hardship and adversity which connects both extremities."
– Hegel

Many people know the benefits of endeavour and adversity intuitively to forge character and fortitude, but why do so few of us commit to the pursuit of activities that lead to this treasure?

Perhaps it is because they are not prepared to be without comfort, even for a short time. The comfortable couch has produced few explorers, but many prefer to watch others from the safety of this comfort zone. In contrast, others grasp the mantle of exploration and the rawness of the wild adventure. Perhaps over time, we've been seduced by the television to become passive observers of the experiences of other more daring souls, living our adventures through the projection of fantasy fuelled by TV.

Have you ever watched a survival programme on television and desired to experience the rawness of nature?

Mountains can be cold, dangerous and unforgiving, especially to the unprepared and the uneducated – but they do forge character like no textbook or television programme could ever hope to do. There is something ancient and mystical about the time I have spent in the wilderness, almost like an echo from my ancestors, reminding me we were once conditioned and hardened away from the comfort of modernity. Something whispers to your soul about what you can do when placed in such inspiring places. There is a condition that climbers often refer to as 'office hands' – a condition of 'soft hands' which can only be created in the absence of cold weather and hard, brutal, unforgiving rock. Climbers who are out constantly develop hands which may be rough and callused, but are incredibly resilient and robust. Perhaps, as a species, we've collectively got 'office hands' of the entire body and soul?

Rest assured, there is no need to begin this journey with nature with an Everest summit attempt! Just the simple, yet powerful act of going out into nature and experiencing the wilderness at any level is without a doubt good 'soup for the soul'. The bonus is it will start to undo the 'office hands' you might have inadvertently created by too much comfortable living.

Reflection: I do hope that you, the reader, takes away from these chapters the spirit of adventure and adversity. If you're reading this in the first place it means you have something of an 'adventurous' nature, and if you haven't, the greatest triumph I could ever hope for is to encourage you to go to the wilderness and experience for yourself what I describe with words.

There can be no pearl, without first the continued irritation of the oyster.

CHAPTER 30

If Not Now, When?

"It is all one to me where I begin;
for I shall come back again."
– Parmenides

It's easy to find excuses in life for pretty much anything you *don't* want to do. Our brains are evolutionarily hard-wired to stay in places of known safety. It's the reason you always sit in the same seat in a classroom, park in the same bay at Tesco's and, when possible, walk the same route to the shops. Our limbic emotional brain doesn't like 'new' and it dislikes 'the unknown' even more.

The temptation to stay in bed on a cold morning when the harsh wind beats against the window is hard to overcome – it takes commitment and resilience. One approach is to find the reason to do what you want to do, rather than the more straightforward excuse not to. From previous chapters, we know that committing to the task in hand brings rewards, as such things often do. Still, it is about overcoming the sometimes-irresistible urge to remain in a position of comfort. Look for the reasons to get up and go rather than the excuses to stay where you are.

Acta non verba.

As with most of this book's elements, whether it be from Stoic Philosophy or modern psychology, it does take the magic ingredient that binds such things together – commitment. I cannot overstate the importance of applying discipline to each chapter of this book. The intellectual understanding means nothing without practical application, and it is in the deeds that we find the true treasure, not the words.

Out of the night that covers me, black as the pit from pole to pole,
I thank whatever gods may be for my unconquerable soul.
In the fell clutch of circumstance I have not winced or cried aloud.
Under the bludgeoning of chance my head is bloody, but unbowed.
Beyond this place of wrath and tears looms but the horror of the shade,
And yet the menace of the years finds and shall find me unafraid.
It matters not how straight the gate, how charged with punishments the scroll,
I am the master of my fate, I am the captain of my soul.

Invictus by William Ernest Henley

Reflection: Life can be very straightforward sometimes and very complicated at other times; this will not come as a shock to you, I'm sure. Consider every decision you've ever made. It is in its very pure form a simple binary choice. You're either moving towards something you desire, or away from something you fear. You are your choices, and you're the cumulative result of all the choices you've made to this point. Like me, I'm sure some of these choices have been good and brought you to reward and others you might have changed given the opportunity. When you chose to buy this book, you moved toward something you desired, and whenever you decide to stay in bed, you move away from what you fear – discomfort and effort.

They are all your choices, and you have to own them regardless of the outcome.

CHAPTER 31

Look Through the Window

"Out of your vulnerabilities will come your strength."
– Sigmund Freud

There is a famous developmental model called the Johari Window which first came to prominence through Joseph Luft's book, 'Of Human Interaction'. In the model, you have a window separated into four quadrants:

- Quadrant 1 – The Arena Window: This window represents parts of your personality that are open to others, as well as being in your awareness.

- Quadrant 2 – The Façade Window: This window represents parts of your personality that you prefer to keep to yourself.

- Quadrant 3 – The Blind Window: This represents parts of your personality that you're unaware of, but others notice.

- Quadrant 4 – The Unknown Window: This represents parts of your personality yet to be discovered and explored and commonly known as 'hidden potential'.

The goal of exploring your mind, reflecting and then accepting feedback (from those you trust) expands your understanding of yourself. This self-reflection, feedback and disclosure will lead to the expansion of quadrants 2 and 3 which reveal the yet to be discovered 'hidden potential' in the Unknown Window of quadrant 4. As you may recall from Chapter 28, The ancient Greek philosophers epitomised this quality with the Delphic maxim 'Gnothi Seauton' or 'Know Thyself'.

This concept of exploring 'the self' can sometimes be uncomfortable, and for this reason, many people spend their lives in quadrants 1 and 2. Without disclosure and feedback, they rarely develop past their present point. Added to this, genuine self-reflection and honest feedback can be challenging to accept when trust between both parties is not established.

Reflection: When reading this, does it make you wonder about your hidden potential? Utilise this model by drawing the four quadrants on a piece of paper and working with someone you trust to explore the unknown potential you undoubtedly have inside. You must be prepared to accept feedback, which can be challenging, as well as have the courage to disclose.

	Known to self	Not known to self
Known to others	Arena	Blind Spot
Not known to others	Facade	Unknown

CHAPTER 32

Get Out of Your Own Way

"To think and to be is the same thing."
– Parmenides

Consider for a moment *where* are you today? Consider also *who* are you today? The original existential questions of philosophy were *who* are we, *where* do we come from, and *why* are we are here? Strictly from a physics perspective, the atoms that comprise your body were created from an exploding star spewing carbon randomly throughout the galaxy. You are the distant descendent from a supernova event that happened billions of years ago, and in line with the law of entropy your conscious matter will return to the universe from which it was born. To cap off our cosmic family tree, that star's creation originated from the fusion of hydrogen and helium, which in turn would have been created at the big bang event around 14 billion years ago. What a journey it's been to arrive at you. Elizabeth Howell so wonderfully explores this concept in her 2017 blog for space.com

- Humans Really Are Made Of Stardust, a New Study Proves.

The conclusion of this is that we are merely a coalesced carbon community with a mysterious and miraculous ability to emerge consciousness from what should be conscious-less matter. Giving rise to our ability to not only think, but have awareness of our thinking, and via this process become further aware that we not only *are* but we are also *being*; cogito ergo sum.

One way of understanding our existence is to confine it to the boundaries of our perceived reality. We have a limited time on this earth, which by causation only permits us to achieve so much within the confines of the most finite of all resources – time.

Does destiny bind us to effect, or do we bind destiny to cause?

There is a polarity to this mindset though, and depending on your perspective of time, you could also be limitless, or more specifically, you're only *limited* by you. Most of the goals of modern philosophy and coaching are to enable the person to 'get out of the way of themselves'; in other words, remove their self-limiting and self-deprecating beliefs.

The actual head-shaker part of this is that most people are unaware of their own limiting beliefs, so there is little hope of them ever getting out of the way of themselves – it's akin to trying to explain to a fish what water is. A good starting point though is constant self-reflection.

Every being in the Universe
is an expression of the Tao.
It springs into existence,
unconscious, perfect, free,
takes on a physical body,
lets circumstances complete it.
That is why every being
spontaneously honours the Tao.

Lao Tzu

Reflection: Start to examine your beliefs about yourself – good and bad. Your beliefs and language do not describe your reality, more accurately they predict it. Do not imprison yourself within the confines of these limiting beliefs as they will resolutely guard the keys to your potential if left unexamined.

CHAPTER 33

Get to Work!

"Pleasure in the job puts perfection in the work."
– Aristotle

Modernity has changed our perception of work, and indeed also our perception of the meaning of work. Throughout our history we have been ready to sacrifice ourselves for a higher purpose, leading a 'good' life personified by servitude in accordance with the rules of the book, whichever book that may be. The celestial reward for a life of sacrifice and denial would be a place in heaven for eternity.

As time went on though, and with the relative decline of religion (especially in the West), we have exchanged an insignificant role in the grand play of universal existence for a more central and significant role in the minor game of our immediate and personal existence. The Aristotelian philosophy which shaped the religious world view has been questioned by science, and in doing so has sown the seeds of doubt in the minds of humankind.

Pink Floyd famously wrote, *"Did you exchange a walk-on part in the war, for a lead role in the cage?"*

The consequence of this mindset shift is we have forgotten the true reward of 'putting our nose to the grindstone'. It is perhaps unfair to characterise and generalise everyone within this singular description, but I do, nonetheless, believe there has been a significant decline in the appreciation of honest labour. The reality we currently occupy is one of instant gratification, rewards without toil, and a final destination without the heroes' journey that precedes. We desire the 'noun' but we're not always prepared to carry out the 'verbs' that pave the road to the 'noun'. It is the curse of modernity and more specifically symptomatic of our Western culture. Destination minus hardship is the preferred option.

I consider myself very fortunate to have had the opportunity to spend time with highly successful people. Whether in business, sport, the military or adventuring, I have had the chance to learn from some of the planet's leading minds in all these different arenas. There is, without surprise, a commonality between them all.

They commit themselves to the relentless pursuit of their goal each day, regardless of external influences.

Reflection: Finding pleasure in your task changes the perception of the task; this is achieved by being aware of your lens once again. How you look at something determines the meaning you ascribe to the observation and changes the experience of completing it. Approach any task with this mindset, and it will transform your perception of the work you undertake. You can find pride in anything if you look deeply into it.

A man in prison desires to be free.

A free man desires to be rich.

A rich man desires contentedness.

A content man desires nothing.

Read the next chapter to understand more about this…

CHAPTER 34

The Circle of Life

Once there lived a quarryman who toiled day after day. He smashed his sledgehammer and pickaxe against the hard rock day-after-day, relentlessly. It did not matter the weather above his head or how tired he was; the nature of his task was demanding on his body and mind. Often, while working, the quarryman would bitterly complain to the heavens about the hand he had been dealt by fate. The cold rain and bitter winds would especially exacerbate his woes. One day, as he smashed repeatedly against the rock while the harsh rain beat against his soul, he complained bitterly once more.

"Why oh why has fate oppressed me, why could I have not been afforded riches and comfort? I am so powerless and poor, working day upon day in these terrible conditions!"

As he complained, a magical genie appeared next to him and pronounced, "So, if you were to become a rich man with money and wealth, you would then be content with your power?" Without a moment of doubt, the quarryman replied, "Of course! What more could there be for a man to desire but the wealth and power?"

The magical genie clicked his fingers and the quarryman became a rich man. He awoke in a penthouse apartment in a massive four-poster bed with rich silk sheets with all the money he could have imagined in his bank. The quarryman who became a rich man was now content.

One day the rich man heard a huge carnival taking place in the streets below. He went out onto his penthouse's balcony to observe the commotion. Watching, the rich man could see crowds lining the streets below waving patriotic flags of the kingdom, and soldiers following a marching band in parade dress followed by the cavalry. Finally, a golden carriage with eight glorious white horses appeared, the king and queen within. As they waved to the cheering crowds, looking regal beyond the rich man's wildest imagination, the rich man instantly felt a sense of powerlessness.

He compared himself to the king and started to complain once more. "I have nothing in comparison with this king below, for I may have some wealth but the king has castles and a kingdom to rule, with loyal subjects and immeasurable wealth which fills his vaults. I have nothing, and am nothing, compared to the king!"

Once again, the magical genie appeared. "So, if you were to have a castle, kingdom and crown with loyal subjects and immeasurable wealth in your vaults, you would be content with your power?"

The rich man replied sharply, "Of course! What more could any man desire apart from the things you describe? I would be a content king forever with my kingdom and riches!"

Instantly the genie clicked his fingers and the quarryman, who became a rich man, awoke as a king with a castle, crown, loyal subjects, a kingdom as far as the eye could see, and a vault full of gold and jewels. The king was now finally, wholly content.

Some weeks passed and the king was enjoying all that his kingdom had to offer. Spring surrendered to summer and the sun began to beat down on the king's kingdom. Day after day, then week after week, the sun shone constantly without respite. Rivers began to dry, lakes receded, and the tenant farmers from all around the kingdom started to worry as their crops failed due to the relentless heatwave. Still, the sun continued, oblivious to any human prayers for rain. Soon the king's subjects began to protest at the castle's gates, demanding the king do something as he was the God-appointed ruler of the kingdom. The king felt powerless against the unrelenting power of the sun. Looking out across his kingdom, the king started to complain bitterly, "I have no power against the might of the sun! My crown, my gold, my jewels and my castle are all worthless underneath the might of the sun. Why can I not have the power of the sun?"

The genie again appeared and asked the king, “So, if you become a radiant sun with all the power and energy of Sol, you’ll be content?”

The king replied, “Of course, if I was the God Sol, what more could there be than to rule all of the Cosmos with my energy?”

The quarryman, who became a rich man, who became a king, was now a burning sun in the sky, providing energy and power for all around.

The sun was now wholly content with his power, until one day, some deep, dark rain clouds covered the kingdom below. The sun tried to break through the clouds, but the rain persisted beneath, and after a while, the sun became frustrated once more and felt powerless against the rain cloud.

He complained; “This is terrible for I have no power against these deep, dark and powerful rain clouds and try as hard as I might, I cannot even for a moment break past them. I feel so powerless. If only I were a powerful rain cloud for it is water that provides life to all beneath!”

As before, the magical genie appeared and asked, “So, if you were a cloud with the power of water, you would finally be content?”

And, as before, the sun replied, "Of course! What more power is there in the universe than to be the source of all life – water?"

Once again, the genie clicked his fingers, and it became so. The quarryman, who became a rich man, who became a king, who became a sun, was now a vast, dark, imposing rain cloud. The cloud then rained, and rained, and rained, fully exercising his new-found power. One day the cloud noticed some granite rocks embedded in a riverbed below. After observing the rocks, the cloud decided to send a biblical torrent of rain into the mountains, which cascaded downhill and smashed into the rocks in the riverbed, but the rocks held. So, the cloud rained even more, and more, and more, yet the rocks remained solid and resolute against everything the cloud tried. The cloud felt utterly powerless.

"Why can I not be as strong as this granite? My water is brushed off with ease and no matter how much I rain down, these rocks withstand it all. Why can I not have the strength and power of these granite boulders?"

Immediately the genie clicked his fingers again, and the quarryman, who became a rich man, who became a king, who became the sun, who became a rain cloud, finally became a huge block of granite.

Finally, he was now content with his power until the Quarryman approached in the rain one day.

Reflection: One of the primary pursuits of Stoicism is to rid oneself of desire. The bondage of want can handcuff a person to the future at the sacrifice of the present. There will always be more money, a bigger house, a newer car and a more expensive watch. As Professor Shawn Achor suggests with his research on happiness for Harvard University, only about 10% of your happiness can be determined by what you possess. In reality, the other 90% Is entirely what happens Inside the mind.

Credit: The Magic Of The Metaphor – Nick Owen

CHAPTER 35

The Eagle and The Chicken

"The worst of all deceptions is self-deception."
– Plato

There is a small farm on the border between France and Switzerland that sits in Mont Blanc's shade. The farmer who lives there looks after his livestock, of which some are chickens that spend their days scratching and pecking the courtyard floor in search of seeds. The farmer also happens to be a very able and keen climber, spending much of his spare time in the mountains exploring new routes to satisfy his appetite for adventure.

One hot summer's day, the young farmer decided to take an afternoon climb once his chores were complete. He worked with purpose and intent during the morning to allow him the window to complete a new climb and safely return home from the summit. After lunch he set off with his small rucksack with basic supplies, climbing shoes and rope for the hike to the climb's start, which was in the next valley over.

The climbing was challenging and the views extraordinary across the alpine backdrop. As the young climber ascended, searching for secure foot and hand placement, he came across an abandoned eagle's nest. On closer inspection there appeared to be a single remaining egg and with no sign of a mother, the climber had a difficult decision to make. Leaving the egg would mean its certain death but should he take the egg from its natural habitat? The climber decided he would offer the egg a chance of survival, albeit a slim one. He carefully removed the egg from the abandoned nest and placed it gently into his small rucksack, wrapping it inside his jumper for added protection.

For the rest of the route, the climber considered his options to give the eagle's egg the best chance of survival. After much deliberation, he decided that he would place the egg with one of the nurturing hens on his farm once he returned. The walk-off seemed to take longer as the climber was acutely aware of the fragile egg inside his rucksack. He took his time to ensure the egg didn't break. Eventually, he arrived back at his small farm and placed the egg with the mother hen for protection. He then stepped back and observed. Although at first confused, the hen quickly accepted the larger eagle's egg as if one of her own.

As time went by, nature took its course and eventually all the eggs started to hatch one by one, including the baby eagle. As the baby eagle slowly adjusted its eyes, it looked around as the other chickens looked on. He noticed that the chickens walked up and down the courtyard scratching and pecking the floor for seeds, so the baby eagle imitated this. With only other chickens to observe, and no mirror to look at his reflection, the baby eagle became convinced he was also a chicken. The baby eagle walked like a chicken, pecked like a chicken, and even crowed in the morning – just like a chicken. As time went by the young eagle, that thought it was a chicken, was pecking away with the other chickens in the courtyard. Suddenly he noticed a shadow of a mighty bird in the yard. Looking up toward the sky, the eagle that thought it was a chicken noticed a simply majestic and stunning bird circling effortlessly high above. Without even the need to use its vast wings, the bird sailed on the thermals, viewing all that was below. It was the king of the sky, a mature adult eagle.

Having never before witnessed anything of such power, grace and beauty, the young eagle who thought it was a chicken could not take its eyes off the bird high above in the sky. Soon, the adult eagle swooped into the adjacent valley and out of sight. The young eagle that believed itself to be a chicken wondered what it might be like to be an eagle, then returned to scratching the floor and pecking for seeds – because that is what chickens do.

Credit: The Magic of the Metaphor – Nick Owen.

Reflection: We all sit within the boundaries of our self-limiting beliefs. My obsession has always been with hidden potential and exploring ways of helping my clients to release It. The first step with this is always awareness. Change requires this as a prerequisite. An easy way to understand this concept is to explore the things you've always wanted to do, but never found the courage to commit to. In these unfulfilled desires there must be some limiting thinking that prevents you from taking the plunge.

CHAPTER 36

Stoic Principle – Get the Work Done

"Difficulties strengthen the mind, as labour does the body."
*– **Plato***

The Brooklyn Bridge is one of the most iconic sights in New York and a feat of 19th-century engineering that forever changed modern bridge construction. Renowned engineer, John Roebling, envisaged a bridge that would connect Manhattan Island with Brooklyn, spanning the East River. The bridge's story is one of endeavour and adversity, perseverance and determination, ingenuity and courage, all wrapped up in an outright desire to get the work done regardless of the sacrifice. It is a story of a bridge that not only spanned water, but also spanned generations of the same family.

It took ten years of lobbying by Roebling before he finally won approval to begin construction in 1867, with a further fourteen years to build the bridge itself. Before the main construction began, a docking barge crushed Roebling's foot. He contracted tetanus and tragically died one week later before the main project began. The chief engineer's role then passed to his thirty-two-year-old son, Washington Roebling, who accepted the responsibility of completing his father's dream.

Completing the bridge was, at times, perilous work. One of the most hazardous jobs was placing the pressurised pneumatic caissons, which were sunk to a depth of 44.5 feet on the Brooklyn side and 78.5 feet on the Manhattan side. These caissons provided a dry underwater space for workers to dig the bridge's foundations down into the solid rock. Working at these depths often brought on a severe medical condition called 'the bends', caused by moving too quickly to the surface from a high-pressure atmosphere. At the time decompression sickness was not medically understood, so the condition was labelled 'caisson disease'. Washington Roebling himself suffered acute decompression sickness.

By 1872, five years into the project, Washington Roebling was still at the foundation stage of the bridge construction, and he was bed stricken and with limited communication ability. As John had passed away and Washington was severely ill with little hope of meaningful recovery, the project looked set to collapse. Many of the naysayers who had proclaimed its impossibility for years were calling for the abandonment of the doomed Brooklyn Bridge.

However, they had not counted on the resolve and tenacity of Washington and his wife, Emily.

Emily stepped in to continue the construction, becoming the Project Manager and Chief Engineer. She developed a communication method with her husband, Washington, to continue the project against all odds. In 1876 work was completed on the colossal bridge towers, which measured 277 feet above the waterline. With the buildings now complete, the installation of the four main cables could begin. Using John Roebling's patent from thirty years prior, they were the longest and heaviest cables ever constructed, weighing over 3,500 tons and containing 14,000 miles of wire. Finally, after fourteen years of construction, the bridge was opened on May 24th, 1883. Starting with John, then Washington, and finally Emily, it took the determination of three family members and nearly three decades to complete the task.

Reflection: The world is overflowing with unfinished projects, unfulfilled commitments and unrealised dreams. To get anything worthwhile done, it takes the qualities shown by the Roeblings when completing the Brooklyn Bridge. Get started, keep going, see it through to completion.

CHAPTER 37

What You Do in The Dark Defines How You Are in The Light

"The beginning is the most important part of work."
– Plato

I consider myself hugely fortunate to have observed many high performing human beings from many different backgrounds and industries. From military Special Forces to business leaders, and even Olympic and World Champion athletes from various sports. I have enjoyed the privilege of observing and learning from these high performers.

If you watch enough people closely enough, you begin to notice common patterns in their behaviour, mindset and approach over time, regardless of the context. Whether preparing for an Olympic final or building a successful business from scratch, the commonalties remain the same. One trait that is always present in successful people is the ability to do two things:

1. Start.
2. Work in the dark.

These might at first appear simple things, but never confuse simplicity for ease. The most straightforward formulas can be the most effective, just like Einstein's and Newton's famous formulas.

Let's examine Newton's formula and use it as an analogy for getting work done.

$F=ma$

This is Newton's Second Law and means the force (F) acting on an object is equal to the mass (m) of an object multiplied by its acceleration (a). In short, it takes energy, or effort, to create a force sufficient enough to move an object, but once the energy is transferred the object will remain in motion until acted upon by another equal or greater force.

It takes effort to get going, but once you're away, you have momentum on your side.

This formula is relevant when understanding procrastination. Have you ever delayed starting a job until the point where it becomes critical, taking this inaction nearly past the point of no return? Once the project becomes vital, there is always a trigger which initiates the start (F) and once the energy is transferred into the project (m), you start working with purpose and speed (a). The difference with high performers is they transfer the energy immediately and get up to maximum acceleration with their project, whether it's training for an event, launching a business or preparing a presentation.

Reflection: Success is always cultivated behind closed doors and in darkness, usually with few observers. It is carved out with no audience and often with little encouragement. Turn up daily, get started, create momentum, then maintain that momentum when nobody is watching.

Get started and work in the dark.

CHAPTER 38

Let Go or Be Dragged

"To accept without arrogance, to let go with indifference."
– Marcus Aurelius

Do you have regret in your life? Do you spend time reflecting on the things you shouldn't have done, or could have done? How much time do you surrender reminiscing about your past?

Finally, what, aside from reflection, have you done to put right the situation?

We don't laugh at the same joke a thousand times, so why do we feel sad repeatedly about the same event?

If we can learn to accept the good things that come our way without arrogance, can we not learn to let go of negative things with the indifference as Marcus Aurelius describes above?

I am not for a moment saying we should ignore the times when our behaviour and actions have fallen out of alignment with our core values and beliefs. It is suitable to reflect and self-examine our actions, especially when these behaviours fall short of our accountable standards. I am also not suggesting this is an easy task to do, given the blessing and curse of self-awareness and self-reflection.

Guilt is an excellent example of when self-reflection can become self-defeating. Most of us have experienced the all-consuming effect that guilt can wage on our private thoughts.

I carried an incredible amount of guilt with me for nearly ten years. It centred around my behaviour towards someone I cared deeply about and subsequently mistreated. Guilt is like a weed in the garden of your thoughts. At first, imperceivable, then mistakenly thought manageable, before finally mutating from irritable nuisance to constant persecutor. I had tried many ways to overcome this guilt, all undertaken by myself. Nothing worked though. That was until a coaching session in 2010 when I volunteered for a demonstration during my NLP Master Practitioners training of a technique called Parts Integration. During this technique, I let go of my guilt. I acknowledged that my behaviour was wrong, but nonetheless let go of the guilt. I learned for the first time that the conflict I had inside me could be resolved at an unconscious level rather than all the other approaches I had undertaken, which were entirely conscious; and up until that point unsuccessful. I could know I was wrong consciously yet let go of the guilt unconsciously.

If you were to fall from a horse, would you hold onto the reins, allowing it to drag you across the ground? Or would you simply accept you had fallen and let go of the reins? You can accept that you did something to cause your fall at some point in time, then learn from it and move on with humility.

It often saddens me when I work with clients who are holding the reins from events that have happened many years before, finding themselves being emotionally dragged by the event. This is not for one second to devalue the event itself, but pose yourself this question:

"Would my life be enriched if I were to let go of the event and stop being dragged?"

Reflection: Examine the events from your past that still occupy your thoughts, especially if they invoke negative emotions. Ask yourself, "Can I change this, or can I take action to make right anything that needs correcting?"

If you can change something, then take action. If you cannot, let go of the reins.

CHAPTER 39

Our strength is made perfect in weakness (Corinthians 12:9)

"No man has the right to be an amateur in the matter of physical training. It is a shame for a man to grow old without seeing the beauty and strength of which the body is capable."
– Socrates

Our bodies are, in some part, governed by the inheritance of our genetics. It is improbable that I would have ever become an Olympic weightlifter with the body composition and genetics I inherited from my parents. This insignificant fact does not for one second preclude me benefiting from lifting weights though.

Our bodies are incredible, they truly are. We only limit their physical ability with our own beliefs about our psychological capability. Everyone is capable of greatness that is not attached to winning competitions or climbing a mountain (or a hill), paddling a raging river (or a still pond), completing a marathon (or a 5k park run/walk), or committing to a long pilgrimage to Santiago De Compostela in Northern Spain (or walking to the shops). No matter your current situation or condition, you can make positive steps forward. No matter the step's size, just commit to moving forwards and taking positive action.

Occasionally, when considering physical capability, we focus on Olympians and world champions. There are numerous examples of athletes, who are not necessarily Olympians, achieving goals previously thought impossible.

It only takes the unwavering belief of one person with the courage to follow their dream that dares to challenge a collective paradigm – the audacity of hope.

One of my favourite examples of challenging and changing a collective paradigm is the incredible Chris Nikic from Florida. Chris is a twenty-one-year-old triathlete, who happens to have Down's Syndrome. In 2020, he became the first person with Down's Syndrome to finish the gruelling Ironman distance triathlon. In truth, he was also the first ever to enter an Ironman. He finished the final element, the twenty-six-mile marathon, with sixteen minutes to spare wearing a t-shirt emblazoned with '1% better' on the front – the philosophy his father had instilled within him throughout his life.

Constant 1% gains will eventually arrive you at your dreams.

The official Ironman Twitter account tweeted: "You have shattered barriers while proving without a doubt that anything is possible."

Reflection: Wherever you are today reading this, whatever your situation or condition you find yourself in, do not concern yourself with what you cannot do, focus only on what you can do – then do it with the purpose of Chris Nikic!!

"Cycling never gets easier; you just go faster."
– Greg Lemond 3x Tour De France Champion

CHAPTER 40

Stoicism Virtue 3/4 – Courage

"Throw me to the wolves, and I will return leading the pack."
– Seneca

Throughout history, there are marvellous examples of courage we can all admire and hopefully learn from. Sometimes these incredible acts of colossal bravery can distract us from what I believe the Stoics referred to as one of the four virtues – courage.

There is the courage we feel when confronted with a seemingly impossible or daunting task, finding the resources deep within to step forward, no matter the adversity. These are once-in-a-lifetime events when the randomness of chance places a person in a specific place, at a specific time. This is what I refer to as 'once-in-a-lifetime courage'.

Also, there are those examples of courage which are less grand, yet far more frequent. The daily opportunities to step up in certain situations. This is what I refer to as 'everyday courage'.

Everyday courage is performing those small and seemingly insignificant acts which will never be written into a Hollywood movie, yet unfold the tapestry of our reality gradually. The time you saw something wrong and dared to speak out, led by your values and beliefs. Or the wrong that you inflicted on someone else that took courage to publicly correct, when doing nothing is often the easier option. It is that time you defended someone who does not have the ability (or perhaps courage) to defend themselves against a foe.

This everyday courage is remarkable because life will always provide ample opportunities to practice this virtue, unlike once in a lifetime courage. There are often wrongs to right, people to defend, and mistakes to correct. This is where I believe true courage resides, and it lives in us all. The Stoics believed that doing what was right sometimes took courage, but should always be done, nonetheless.

Reflection: As I write this chapter, I reflect on the times when I did not have the courage to act following my moral compass. Unfortunately, there have been too many entirely for my liking. I can also say that over the years, I have worked hard to develop the courage to follow my compass regardless of the adversity it brings. I have always greatly admired uncompromising people as they often represent this Stoic virtue with abundance. Unwavering and relentless in their beliefs of what is right and wrong, and unafraid to exercise their integrity should it be called upon.

Are these not the qualities you would like to forge within yourself?

Ask yourself the question; "What injustices have I witnessed recently, no matter how small?"

Also, you can ask; "Do I have any wrongdoings in my past, and do I have the courage to correct them today?"

Finally, remember one last element to understand courage:

Knowing something might hurt and doing it anyway is called courage.

Knowing something might hurt and doing it anyway is also called stupidity.

Wisdom is figuring out which one is which.

CHAPTER 41

Get to Know Your Ego(s)

"In most of our human relationships, we spend much of our time reassuring each other that our costumes of identity are on straight."

– Ram Dass

In his seminal book *Becoming Nobody*, Ram Dass opens the first chapter by describing being born wearing a spacesuit. He expands on how he learned to use his spacesuit, primarily via external feedback about life's rights and wrongs, dos and don'ts. From the earliest age he was encouraged by all of those around him to add badges to his suit and ensure it was always worn correctly, no matter the internal discomfort. He even talks about becoming so attached to his spacesuit he completely forgot he was wearing one. When Dass started to descend into neurosis, he visited a man who also wore a spacesuit with completely different badges to the ones he had acquired, called a therapist. Ram Dass was so impressed by this suit he set about acquiring one he could wear, and when he did, his new suit impressed all his friends and family.

He calls this 'somebody training'.

This concept might seem peculiar to read; after all, we rarely embark on a pursuit to become a 'nobody'. As the saying goes: 'everybody wants to be somebody'.

This continuous pursuit is your ego at work. Perhaps once more, this is the 'more = better' Western paradox at work. You feel as though you need to be a significant somebody, but Ram Dass believes you're already significant and would, in fact, be much happier and content letting go of this ever-lasting pursuit.

Chapter 10 explored the concept of the two 'selves' residing in all of us, the 'Self-Image' (present) and the 'Ideal-Self' (future). If we examine this slightly deeper, and through Ram Dass' teachings, each self is just a spacesuit. One suit that you currently wear, and one suit you're aspiring to wear, only the future suit undoubtedly has more badges. You are *just* you, and will always be *(just)* you, no matter how many badges you accrue along the way. Everything else is your ego and attachment.

Now, I'm not suggesting to you to immediately embark on a spiritual awakening; that would be my ego influencing my writing of those words. I only encourage you to explore the idea of your 'self', which will by the nature of the task undertaken, cause you to illuminate your awareness of your ego.

Our minds can attach meaning within this process of knowing, but the pursuit of letting go is to simultaneously accept all. There is the presence of good and evil in every moment and the absence of both in the same moment.

Reflection: The spirit of the Spartan Agoge was, in essence, to allow the young Spartan children to 'Know Thyself', or in Greek 'Gnothi Seauton'. The more profound question that modern philosophers like Ram Dass are now exploring is whether the self exists at all, and if not, what is left behind in its place? Spending time in quiet reflection is a good starting point in the quest of knowing thyself. Looking back across the previous day and exploring your reactions to everyday situations will bring a new understanding, particularly with regard to the lens through which you see the world.

CHAPTER 42

Drama, Drama, Drama!

"Empty vessels make the loudest sounds."
– Plato

There is a body of knowledge called *Transactional Analysis*, which is a form of psychotherapy developed by Dr Eric Berne. In truth, much of modern psychology has its origins within Greek philosophy, and more accurately Stoicism.

When Dr Berne passed away in 1970, his work was developed further by various contributors, including Stephen Karpman. One of the ideas that Karpman developed was the drama triangle, which is a wonderful model for understanding the psychology of drama and – most importantly – strategies for avoiding it.

Reflect on all the times you've experienced drama in your life. You may notice that there were specific roles within the drama, and these roles required characters.

As an example, we can look at a fictitious scenario of domestic violence. The husband can play the role of 'Persecutor' (P), and the wife will accommodate 'Victim' (V). The police are called to handle the situation, so they enter the triangle as the 'Rescuer' (R). Unfortunately, these roles, by their very nature, exchange and move positions around the triangle with breath-taking fluidity. On arrival at the scene, the policeman (R), after appraising the situation, immediately needs to restrain the husband who occupies the (P) position. In doing so, they exchange roles; the policeman now moves to the (P) position, and the husband moves to (V) in the triangle. This now leaves the wife without a role, and when hearing the distress of her restrained husband, attempts a rescue of her now beleaguered spouse and turns on the policeman. In doing this, she moves to the (R) position for her husband but also the (P) position relative to the policemen who now occupies the (V) position. All of these psychological exchanges could occur in quite literally a blink of an eye.

Reflection: Drama is fed by energy, and the most common mistake is to try and rescue the situation. In so doing, you enter the drama and become part of it. The key is to take the energy out of the drama, which can only be done by remaining calm and avoiding the temptation to either judge (you'll take on the Persecutor position), or pity (you'll take on the Rescuer position). Remain neutral, exercise temperance, and speak calmly only using facts and evidence to support your words. In doing this, you'll remain outside of the triangle.

Reading the Stoics work, I think they intuitively understood this model thousands of years before Karpman so eloquently explained it.

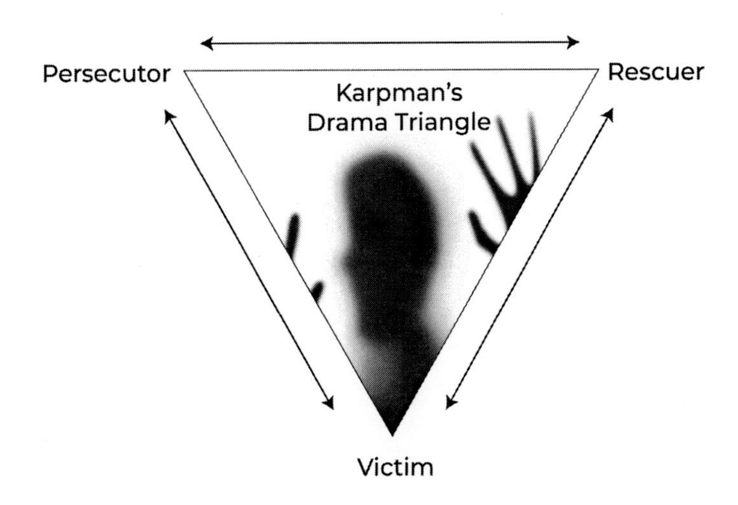

CHAPTER 43

What's Driving Your Behaviour?

"By three methods we may learn wisdom: first, by reflection, which is noblest; second, by imitation, which is easiest; and third by experience, which is the bitterest."
*– **Confucius***

As a child, did you ever dream of being something only to be counselled against the idea with well-intended advice? "You shouldn't study music because you'll never make a living being a musician" or "Don't take dance, you'll never be a dancer" etc. In truth, many of our beliefs are nurtured and shaped in the environment we occupy during the early formative years of our life. Unfortunately, this environment isn't always within our control during these early critical years and this can have a profoundly consequential effect on our adult belief systems. Our core beliefs about what we can or can't do, who we can or can't be, and even what we can or can't have, are shaped early in our life. According to the author Morris Massey, this is during the first 7 years of life, known as the "imprint period" of development.

Consider these three questions for a moment:

Are you *being* who you want to *be*?

Are you *doing* what you want to *do*?

Do you *have* what you want to *have*?

Within my coaching practice, many scenarios are centred around my client's belief in these three areas of *being, doing* or *having*.

Some of my clients have challenges being who they want to be, and in my experience, this often correlates with a self-perceived inability to start things. If you are trapped in a state of eternal indecision, you will most likely never take the steps necessary towards the person you desire to be.

For other clients, their limitations are around doing what they want to do, and this is often reflected professionally with their chosen career. Usually, with this group, the self-perceived inability centres around the courage to change things; they find themselves in an occupation which is more akin to forced labour than a career or vocation.

Finally, I have clients whose primary blockage is having what they want to have but their limitations involve an inability to finish things. This is also referred to as a Sisyphus driver from Greek mythology. Sisyphus cheated Thanatos (God of

Death) three times in life and his punishment for his self-aggrandising craftiness was condemnation to eternal labour. Sisyphus' task was to push a giant boulder uphill, however, just as Sisyphus was about to reach the summit, the boulder slipped from his grasp and rolled back down the hill, forcing him to repeat the task forever.

Much of our conditioning is well-intended and usually comes to us from a desire of protection and preservation. The unforeseen consequence of this well-intended advice is the subsequent development of self-limiting beliefs about who we are, what we can do and, finally, what we can have. These self-limiting beliefs are mostly unconscious unless we take the time to examine ourselves, but they appear within our language and unwittingly shape our observable results. Have you noticed how at times the same result can repeat over and over, even against your will?

Reflection: Listen to your words and carefully examine your language, which will no doubt contain these subtle self-limiting beliefs. Your language does not describe who you are; it determines who you are.

"Give me a child until he is seven and I will show you the man."

– Aristotle

CHAPTER 44

You Can't Chase Two Rabbits at the Same Time

"The successful warrior is the average man with laser-like focus."
– Bruce Lee

It can sometimes appear the entire world is busy. From CEOs and entrepreneurs, to homemakers and even students, 'busy' is the most honourable badge to wear. We want to focus on the seductively capitalist dream of increased productivity providing wind in our sails, yet we are simultaneously inhibited by the constant distractions dragging us back like an invisible anchor. Information and distraction surround us and arrest our senses like no other time in humankind's history. The world sparkles like a shiny coin to a magpie. The champions of the future need not worry about access to information; that future is bathed in information for everyone to access. They will most likely separate themselves from their competitors by creating an absence of digital distractions. Even as I write this chapter, I am continually being seduced by these alluring distractions, whether from my email notifications, or the temptation to check how my Facebook / LinkedIn / Instagram posts are performing. It can sometimes appear as though our cognitive output is conspired against by the very technology that's intended to increase productivity and efficiency. Like the corporate lie sold to us at the turn of the 20th century that email would reduce our workload, only for the reality to be anything but the initial promise.

As Daniel Goleman incisively writes: "Starve your distractions, feed your focus."

Part of the problem resides in our erroneous belief that we can multi-task with any kind of effectiveness. We cannot. Although marvellous, our brains do not work like computers insomuch that they do not dual-process multiple tasks simultaneously. Now you might read this and disagree. But in truth what we do is alternate our focus between tasks, switching back and forth, sometimes with incredible speed but still switching, nonetheless. The ability to focus on a singular task is becoming a distant skill, lost in the ocean of 'busyness' and the misplaced false economy of multi-tasking.

The natural window of high-quality focus and concentration is around 90 minutes (maximum) and is embedded within our daily Ultradian Rhythm. After this 90-minute period, our minds begin to lose focus, attention becomes diluted, and decisions become more laborious. Subsequently, distractions become more prevalent. At its worst conclusion this is where accidents can happen from focus fatigue. To starve distraction, remove anything from your immediate space which might take away your focus. All of your senses can be distracted from their tasks, so if you want focus and concentration, you must create the supporting conditions for this.

For example, when writing this book, I moved my phone away from where I was working and turned it to silent. I closed any unnecessary windows on my laptop and made sure all social media pages were closed in my browser bar. One of my strategies was to have music that supported concentration; for me, piano concertos played quietly worked perfectly. To feed my attention, I ensured the environment I chose to write in was conducive to concentration and focus. I created minimum word goals per session and only allowed myself to stop once these goals were met. In between the focused sessions, I checked emails, made calls or browsed social media. The result of this was around 2,000 / 2,500 words written per day. Take care of the words and the chapters will look after themselves. It is all achieved by focus and concentration.

Reflection: Improving focus takes practice, and our world is ergonomically designed to prevent us from creating the conditions. Understand this and control your environment paying attention to any possible distractions. Finally, where possible, minimise your focus time to less than ninety minutes with a twenty-minute mental relaxation period. The aim is to be productive, not busy – they are not the same thing!

CHAPTER 45

Learn Like You'll Live Forever, Live Like You'll Die Tomorrow

"Cogito ergo sum."
– Rene Descartes

The words written above are perhaps the most famous philosophical words: "I think; therefore, I am." In truth, there is a lesser-known part which comes before this: *"Dubito ergo cogito,"* which means "I doubt; therefore, I think."

Growing up on the Isle of Man during the 1990s, I attended Queen Elizabeth II High School on the west coast of the island. I think it would be fair to characterise myself as a 'less than exemplary student'. Like many children, I was given a metaphorical badge to wear by my teachers, obviously in part due to my day-to-day behaviour. The badge I was gifted read 'sporty not bright', perhaps with a secondary badge of 'disruptive'. Not for one second do I proportion blame on my teachers for these labels though. I embraced them entirely, internalised them, and set about the task of living up to them. In truth I wore these with the pride and valour associated with the bearer of such titles.

There was an unforeseen consequence of this though: I forgot to take the badge off and carried on wearing it far past its usefulness. I had often reinforced this label and further fortified my teacher's predictions rather than examined their validity. It wasn't until approaching my 30th birthday, and some fourteen years after leaving school, that I picked up my first book and began a reading journey that eventually brought me here today – writing my own book. It took the belief and encouragement of someone else while on a course I attended in the RAF to suggest to me that my boundaries and beliefs that limited myself existed only in my mind. I was a prisoner of my self-beliefs. This man's name was Mark Lovatt and he was the officer commanding of Joint Service Adventure Training Centre (JSATC) in Lllanwryst, North Wales. He first encouraged me to explore the more developmental elements of being a Royal Air Force Adventure Training Instructor (ATI). I began by reading Stephen Covey's *7 Habits of Successful People*, and I have not relented in the pursuit of knowledge since. I found the books I was reading enthralling and set about at a ferocious pace to catch up on the many lost years believing I lacked intellect. Most surprisingly to me was from the outset I absorbed the information like a sponge soaking water; it appeared I understood the concepts very quickly and retained the contents of these books with shocking ease.

This seemingly innocuous intervention at an advantageous point in time set me off on a personal development journey which would enable me to launch successful businesses, coach some of the world's highest achievers, and even perhaps to become a signed author. In truth, my appetite for learning is as ferocious as my appetite for oxygen – with the need to feed both hungers continually and relentlessly. Reading and learning are the gifts we're all bestowed, but often seem to lack the desire to fully embrace. Books do not discriminate between the rich and the poor and, regardless of social standing, holding a book can provide the same value to every reader, regardless of circumstance.

Perhaps we achieve the first part of Descartes' quote more effectively than the latter part. If you doubt your capacity to learn, you will most likely not commit yourself to start the journey of learning. However, when you move past your doubt, you will realise that the human capacity to learn is nearly unlimited. According to Pyotr Anokhin from Moscow University (also a student of the legendary psychologist Ivan Pavlov), the minimum number of potential thought patterns the average brain can make is the number 1 followed by 10.5 million kilometres of typewritten zeros in this font size! There seems to be very little that's *average* about your brain in this context. Like many elements of this book, it would appear we limit our cognitive abilities, rather than our cognitive capability limit us.

Reflection: Stop telling yourself you can't learn and that you're not intelligent or academic. Most likely it's all bullshit lies you've convinced yourself of at some point in your life. The key to learning is finding something you *enjoy* learning about – when this happens, the rest becomes effortless.

CHAPTER 46

Your Brain is Plastic

"As long as you live, keep learning how to live."
– Seneca

Is it simplicity in nature that sits beneath complexity, or perhaps it is the complexity that resides beneath simplicity? In its most binary reality, nature is either growing or dying; nature doesn't do 'status quo'. The common belief held in science, until relatively recently, was that the human brain stopped growing at the end of adolescence, hence the idea that children are much better learners than adults. We now know for certain that although the brain may stop growing in physical size at a point in time, it does not preclude it from having the capability to continually develop and grow (Kolb, Gibb et al 2010).

In the year 2000, scientists Eleanor A. Maguire, David G. Gadian, Ingrid S. Johnsrude, and Christopher D. Frith released the findings of a study called 'Navigation-related structural change in the hippocampi of taxi drivers'. In this study they examined the brains of London cab drivers who famously take 'The Knowledge' test. Only on successful completion of 'The Knowledge' are they allowed to trade as licensed London Black Cab drivers. There were two groups for the experiment. The first group contained the cab drivers who were all between thirty-two to sixty-two years old (mean age of forty-four), right-handed, with no medical conditions and all had been licensed for over one and a half years at the time of the experiment. The first group's time range to pass 'The Knowledge' ranged from ten months to three and a half years, with a mean average of two years. The second group (the control group) were identical in age range, all right-handed, with no medical conditions. The only common difference was the control group had never studied for 'The Knowledge' in any capacity.

Through the experiment, it was discovered that **"the posterior hippocampi of taxi drivers were significantly larger relative to those of control subjects. Added to this, a more anterior hippocampal region was larger in control subjects than in taxi drivers."**

The posterior hippocampi role in the brain is to facilitate spatial memory in the form of navigation. Studies have found that increased hippocampal volume in relation to brain and body size is present in birds and mammals who require spatial memory for activities such as storing food or location. In summary, any animal that needs to utilise the brain's navigational element will develop increased hippocampi volume as a consequence of undertaking related tasks. Do we have nature or nurture at play here?

The experiment indicates that the aspirant cab drivers studying for 'The Knowledge' placed a demand on this specific part of the brain to grow. Think of it like going to a 'brain gym', but you're only interested in completing bicep curls and disregarding all other body parts. Over time it would not surprise you that your biceps would begin growing in relation to the rest of your body; conversely, you might not expect any significant improvement or gains in any other parts of the body which you choose not to exercise.

This is truly amazing to consider: your brain responds to the stress you place on it via mental challenges by adapting and growing following intensity and frequency.

Our brains have infinitely more capacity to learn than we believe they do, and the ability to make new synaptic connections exists for us all. The idea that you "can't learn a new language", for example, is only a self-limiting belief – you absolutely can as we explored in Chapter 8!

Reflection: The thing you've wanted to learn, but always told yourself you couldn't, you can. London cab drivers were not born with an extraordinary capacity to remember street names and directions across an entire city. However, they did commit to and complete a mental gym programme that forced this part of their brain to grow and develop.

CHAPTER 47

Stoicism Virtue 4/4 – Temperance

"He that is slow to anger is better than the mighty; and he that rules his spirit than he takes a city."
– Proverbs 16:32

Perhaps the most elusive of the virtues of Stoicism for many is the pursuit of temperance or restraint. It can at first appear a relatively straightforward virtue, but our well-documented Western culture's collective record with New Year resolutions speaks volumes about our powers of control and perseverance. In truth, temperance is a virtue that can bring you closer to Zeno, Seneca, Marcus Aurelius, and the other great Stoics of antiquity, perhaps more than any other element. This seemingly straightforward concept of showing restraint in any given situation is easy to apply to the aspects of our life that need little control, but indeed not so easy with the things we *really* desire, but perhaps know we shouldn't.

I can use myself as an example of this. I have always enjoyed having a drink and socialising, and without a doubt, it is a big part of my life. Each year through the Christmas period I perhaps enjoy this element a little *too* much, showing very little restraint compared to other periods of the year. Also, I enjoy running, but often in December, these runs evaporate with the ascension of a toxic cocktail of furious end of year business activity, coupled with outrageously frequent social events. I then arrive at the beginning of January feeling run down and slightly overweight, and I nearly always abstain for a month or so as compensation.

The question is, am I showing temperance?

Well, in part, yes. But also, in part, very much no. It's simple for me to abstain in January because the elements to support my behaviour are now supportive of my goal. There are fewer events to go to and no Christmas parties, and the festive season often leaves many fiscally challenged in January so the opportunity and funds are both reduced. I'm usually unhappy with my appearance, which further motivates me. Also from a business perspective January is often a deep planning month when clearer thinking is needed. This couldn't be further from the previous month for all the opposite reasons. I am writing these words on the January 7th 2021 and have given myself this entire month to gain momentum with this book. Not drinking alcohol is relatively easy in these conditions too as it supports this broader goal and takes very little temperance to achieve.

Showing temperance isn't about sailing while the wind is in your sails. More accurately it's about learning how to sail when a headwind obstructs your progression.

In Tarot, the card representing temperance is nearly always depicted by a person pouring liquid from one cup into another, and often they have one foot placed in water and the other placed on the land. The meaning is interpreted as bringing balance, patience, and moderation into your life.

To truly practice temperance, it would mean moderating my drinking in December, not January, and developing the ability to meet friends socially during the festive period yet also abstain through conscious choice. It is worth interjecting here and clarifying this is not about stopping something you enjoy entirely or developing a 'Grinch-like' trait – it is about discipline, restraint and moderation.

Reflection: Look for areas of your life that could benefit from adding temperance and gently apply these Greek Stoic lessons. As with all the virtues and principles of Stoicism, it takes commitment and perseverance to become masterful of any element. Be mindful of what Marcus Aurelius said though: *"Be tolerant with others and strict with yourself."*

CHAPTER 48

Circles

"The place to begin building any relationship is inside ourselves, inside our circle of influence, our own character."
– Stephen Covey

Principle one in Stephen Covey's best-selling book *The 7 Habits of Highly Successful People* is 'Be Proactive'. One of Covey's models within this initial principle is derived from much older sources, originating once again within Greek Stoicism. This sublime model examines the different circles we have in our life.

Circle of Control: The circle at the centre of the model, which by its very nature is inherently most profound within us, is our *Circle of Control.* These are the elements of our life which we have direct control of and can, by our actions, immediately determine the outcomes of, like the time we go to bed and rise the following morning.

Circle of Influence: The next circle, outside the inner control circle, is our *Circle of Influence.* These are the elements of our life that we can influence if we were to take some positive action, although we don't have complete control. An example being the quality of sleep we achieve between going to bed and rising. The more action undertaken will consequentially bring these elements close to the centre. Conversely, inaction will push them farther toward the outside and into the *Circle of Concern.*

Circle of Concern: The final outer circle is our *Circle of Concern.* This circle contains the elements of our life that we worry and are anxious about, but over which we have no control or influence whatsoever, like the next-door neighbours having a party through the night and ruining the sleep from the previous two examples. Even aspects at the very centre in our *Circle of Control* will over time migrate to this area with inaction.

At the centre of the circle is proactiveness, and as we move from the centre to the outside, it progressively becomes reactive with time.

Reflection: With a straightforward exercise, you can audit these circles quite easily. Take three pieces of A4 paper and draw four large circles within each piece of paper. Label the *Control*, *Influence* and *Concern* circles. Start with the *Control* circle and place into this everything in your life you have direct control over, then complete the same task with the *Concern* circle, placing into it the elements of your life you worry about but have no power over. Finally, do the same with the *Influence* circle. Do this last as sometimes this can be slightly more ambiguous than the previous circles. Once you have completed this, the action you take is to focus on the proactive *Circle of Control* first and foremost, then examine how you can bring the *Circle of Influence* closer to you. Finally, you can acknowledge the elements outside of the circle you cannot control without worrying or stressing unnecessarily over them.

You will mostly like find that the more you focus on the *Circles of Control* and *Influence*, the outside *Circle of Concern* starts to take care of itself.

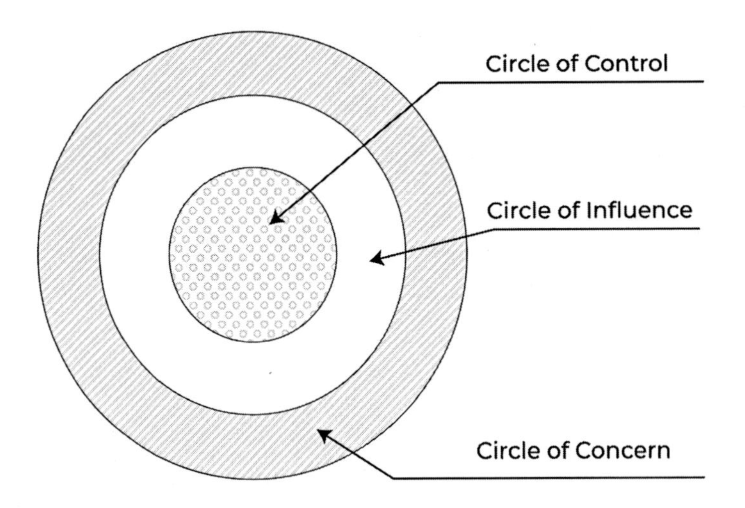
Circle of Control
Circle of Influence
Circle of Concern

CHAPTER 49

Stoic Principle – Find a Role Model

"I will either find a way or make one."
– Hannibal

Hannibal is one of the most revered military tacticians in the history of warfare and, alongside Alexander the Great, most likely the most successful also.

Hannibal's fame emerged from his astounding victories in the Second Punic War between Carthage and Rome. Often hugely outnumbered, Hannibal inflicted crushing defeat after crushing defeat on the Roman Legions. He revolutionised battlefield tactics by turning his enemies' greatest strength into their weakness. In the Romans' case, this was discipline and rigidity. After their loss in the First Punic War, a 9-year-old Hannibal watched as Rome plundered Carthage through levies and taxes in 241 BC after the Carthaginian forces surrendered. 218 BC marked the start of the Second Punic War between the Roman Empire and Carthage. Legend has it that the young Hannibal swore an oath to his father to fight the Romans for his entire life in revenge.

While the First Punic War was predominately about gaining control of Sicily's island, the Second war was triggered in southern Spain. After a succession of stunning victories, Hannibal marched his army, complete with elephants, through the Alps. Although this perilous journey depleted his army considerably, including losing most of his elephants, it did not weaken his ambition to immediately fight with any Roman army presented. Hannibal and his army fought and emphatically won three significant battles over three years, starting in 218 BC at the Battle of Trebia, followed by Lake Trasimene in 217 BC, before finally crushing a vast Roman army at the Battle of Cannae in 216 BC.

Taking to the battlefield, the Roman numbers stood at 86,400 compared to the significantly smaller army commanded by Hannibal numbering approximately 50,000. Incredibly, Hannibal's army only suffered 5,700 fatalities compared to the tremendous losses of the Roman army, which was estimated at 48,200 killed and 19,300 captured, with around 14,000 escaping the battle to return to Rome.

One of the wounded soldiers who escaped the field in Cannae and fled back to Rome was a young general called Publius Cornelius Scipio Africanus. Although defeated at Cannae, he learned from the experience of facing Hannibal.

While recovering from his injuries in Rome, Scipio became obsessed with studying Hannibal's brilliance and tactics.

Finally, after fourteen years of studying Hannibal's battle tactics the now mature Scipio met Hannibal at the Battle of Zama in 202 BC. The Battle of Zama took place in Carthage, and this time the armies were numerically even, which undoubtedly emboldened Hannibal after his emphatic victory fourteen years earlier. Scipio's Roman army inflicted the first devastating defeat on an army led by Hannibal during the entire sixteen-year period of the Second Punic War. Scipio achieved this piece of tactical ingenuity by using the tactics often employed by Hannibal's army.

The student had become the master.

Reflection: If you want to improve in any area of your life, look for a role model who excels and set about the task of modelling excellence. Like Scipio, you might not even like the person you're modelling, but observation, reflection, repetition, and perseverance will eventually get you to the point of mastery.

CHAPTER 50

Stop & Listen

"We have two lives, and the second begins
when we realise we only have one."
– Confucius

The whole world seems in a rush to get somewhere. I suspect you too have perhaps noticed this already, and most likely you have occasionally been caught up in our species' collective urgency.

I am somewhat in a rush to write this book; there is an urgency about my work, for sure!

The odd thing is, as I write these words and cast a glance through the window to the right of my desk, I notice the courtyard outside has the most incredible light dusting of snow. Not snow with any vast amount of depth, just a very gentle, almost understated coating, like when you dust a Victoria sponge cake with icing sugar through a sieve. The beauty of this is truly remarkable. I have lived in this barn for over four years and not until this moment witnessed a morning quite like the one gifted to me today. What is stranger, perhaps, is that I have only noticed this visually arresting sight of nature after 90 minutes of writing this book. Furthermore, had I not been writing this particular chapter, I might never have noticed it! Is this the curse of modernity, to miss these seemingly small, insignificant moments of beauty; the kind of magical moments children seldom miss and seem to continuously pay wondrous attention to?

Life can be busy, that goes without saying, and the busyness will undoubtedly take care of itself. However, your task is to occasionally 'unbusy' yourself for a moment. Stop and concentrate on what's happening around you. And listen, but if you're going to take the time to listen perhaps you will also allow the time to look, hear, smell, and even taste this incredible reality in which we co-create and co-participate.

For example, many of my clients enjoy coffee, as do I. Perhaps you do too? Often, I will ask them the question, "When was your last unforgettable experience of coffee?"

If we love coffee, as we coffee lovers often espouse, then indeed we should treat it in the way that love demands, which is to pay attention to it and savour every element of the experience. Unfortunately, this is not often the case for many, myself included. We often get caught up in the busyness of life and forget that time is not there to occupy our future commitments and attention; it exists only in this singular moment, and our consciousness begets this fundamental principle. The future has not happened and is yet undetermined and unfulfilled. The past exists only in our memories as fragmented synaptic connections, often presenting a subjective partial recollection of the actual objective event for our consciousness to make sense of. If you accept this paradigm, you are forced to make one further acknowledgement with your acceptance. If the only element we experience of reality is the *now,* then perhaps this means all that exists is this *now.* The endless present, literally and figuratively.

There has only ever been now. There is only now. There will only ever be now.

There is only this exact moment, contained precisely within our subjective reality. You and I are not even sharing this moment as author and reader because your *now* has become my *past* and no longer exists for me. While I write this, you are where you are in space and time, but when you read these words I have written today, I will be somewhere else in space and time. Space and time really can chew the mind up!

Reflection: If all we have is the *now,* are we collectively, and individually, making the most of time? Are we squandering these present moments in the cognitive fire of obsession with that which has already passed and that which is yet to come?

CHAPTER 51

The Flood

"We have two ears and one tongue so that we would listen more and talk less."

– Diogenes

There was once a story of a great flood that beset a city many years ago. The combination of rains and storm winds conspired to break the flood barriers of a city that had long danced perilously with the possibility of flooding. As the flood defences began to fail, the city's mayor ordered all residents' immediate evacuation.

First, the mayor sent teams out on foot, wading through rising waters, systematically evacuating each house. Eventually, the team arrived at the house of a very religious man as the water levels approached waist deep. The man refused to leave his house proclaiming to the would-be rescuers, "I shall not leave my house until God sends me the sign that it is time for me to leave. I place my faith with Him entirely and await His sign."

Still, the water levels continued rising, so the mayor sent out another team. This time they were required to take a boat, as the levels were now too high to wade through. Again, they worked thoroughly and systematically until they arrived at the house of the religious man. Despite their best efforts to convince him he once again repeated, "I shall not leave my house until God sends me the sign that it is time to leave. I place my faith only in Him and await His sign."

Finally, with the water level approaching the rooftop of the religious man's house, the mayor sent a helicopter to rescue the remaining resident. Once again, when the helicopter team tried to convince the spiritual man to climb the ladder from the roof he was now stranded upon. He repeated "I shall not leave my house until God sends me the sign that it is time for me to leave. I place my faith only in the Lord and await His sign for me to leave my house."

The water continued to rise, eventually covering the house and tragically drowning the man.

On arrival at the heavenly gates and upon entry from the guardian angel, the now angry religious man demanded an audience with God. The angel pointed his finger toward the elevator and gestured upward higher in the sky. The godly man entered the celestial elevator, and it started rising almost symbiotically with the anger of the man as he approached the top floor.

When the doors finally opened on the very top floor, the man walked with furious intent towards God, asking the question in his final few furious strides. "Why, my Lord, did you let me die on my roof after my years of devotion and service? Why did you not send me a sign? I waited patiently with the unwavering belief you would spare me by giving me a sign!"

God calmly replied, "My son, I first sent men on foot, then I sent more men in a boat, and finally more men with a helicopter. Perhaps you did not look closely enough for the sign?"

Credit: The Magic of the Metaphor – Nick Owen

Reflection: We often wait for a sign to initiate our action: "I'll start the diet next week" or "I'll join the gym in January" or "I'll give up smoking next year". More often than not, kicking these things *we should be doing* down the temporal road encourages a constant extension of the horizon. If not now, when? If not you, who? Don't wait for a sign to initiate action, take action to initiate the sign.

CHAPTER 52

To Find Yourself, Think for Yourself

"Be a free thinker and don't accept everything you hear as truth. Be critical and evaluate what you believe in."
– Aristotle

Sometimes I am completely dumbfounded by modern living. Perhaps this partially explains my obsession to learn the timeless wisdom of antiquity. This world of fake news and misinformation makes me concerned for our future generations. It is already shaping and defining cultures at a speed hitherto never experienced before by humans on earth.

Part of this culture shift is the climate of immediacy that now exists; everything we could want, right here, right now. We desire the 'noun' but don't always want to do the 'verbs' that line the path toward the outcome. For example, many people desire to be rich and wealthy, but not so many are prepared to commit to the relentless work towards this goal, preferring to enter games of chance like the lottery or engage in the 'get rich with minimum effort' promises of the internet. Today we live in a culture of immediacy; waiting for things seems such a distant concept. Social media bombards our senses with what we 'should' be like instead of what we really are like.

My industry of coaching is one of the most severe offenders of digital insanity. I imagine your social media channels are brimming with wealth and success coaches espousing shortcuts to the promised land. Success, money, and how to create the perfect body and mind in four easy steps that takes less than twenty minutes per day – it is madness personified and sails perilously close to outright recklessness.

There are now even coaches for coaches, promising the secrets of how to tap into the golden well of constant clients – the secrets of getting more clients, taught by the coach who has often bypassed the 'getting more clients' stage themselves, and instead jumping to the end where they teach others how to do what they could not do in the first place! It is almost unfathomably obscene when you say it out loud: a coach with very few clients, teaching new impressionable coaches how to get clients.

I think what Aristotle refers to in his quote from the start of this chapter is the ability to cut through this industry's white noise. Listen to your 'inner coach' rather than the constant humdrum of 'internet gurus'. If you have a deep desire to become masterful at anything, then the exchange of time to journey to mastery is the only rite of passage with no shortcuts. Embrace it.

Reflection: Life can be relatively straightforward. It's just like a ball of wool; there is a beginning, an end, and a significant bit in the middle tangled up most of the time. Decouple your mind from the distractions that take you off your path. Do not wake up at 5 am because that's what works for someone else; do that only if it works for you. Every single piece of advice you're exposed to should be examined critically, as Aristotle said eloquently, *"Be critical and evaluate what you believe in."*

This includes these chapters.

CHAPTER 53

The Hubris Trap

"Ego is the anaesthetic that numbs stupidity."
– Booker T. Washington

On January 28th 1986, approximately seventy-three seconds after take-off, the NASA Challenger space shuttle exploded live on American television rocking a nation to the core. In the aftermath of the disaster the president at the time, Ronald Reagan, set up the Rogers Commission to understand the factors which led to the tragedy. For NASA it had been nineteen years and one day since its last comparable tragedy of this magnitude when three astronauts were lost in the Apollo 1 fire of January 27th 1967.

The 256-page *Rogers Commission Report*'s findings were damning, not insomuch as to the specific cause, which was the O-ring rubbers' faulty design in the rockets. These O-rings could not properly seal in extremely cold temperatures and leaked rocket fuel before exploding less than 73 seconds after launch. The fact remains, the engineers of Morton Thiokol Inc. knew of this flaw, Morton Thiokol being the company that produced the rockets that propelled the shuttle into space. The engineers had tried in vain to postpone the launch due to the predicted low temperatures, however, the management of Morton Thiokol were under incredible pressure from NASA executives to greenlight the launch. NASA's pressure was partly due to the appetite to launch the first civilian into space as part of the 'teacher in space' programme. The Challenger shuttle contained Christa McAuliffe who was a schoolteacher from New Hampshire and was chosen from thousands of hopeful teachers to teach a class of American children from space.

The NASA executives and the upper management of Morton Thiokol were accused of systemic hubris in the report.

But what is hubris?

Hubris is the characteristic of excessive confidence or arrogance, which leads a person to believe that they may do no wrong. The consequence of extreme hubris is the inability to listen to others in decision-making processes. When the outcome is favourable, this can be mistakenly passed off as good leadership; when tragedy strikes, it exposes the actual dangers of hubris and its potential consequences.

"When conceived it was a project of almost unimaginable boldness and foolhardiness, requiring great bravura, risking great hubris."
– Simon Winchester, The Professor and the Madman

As with much of today's wisdom, hubris has its origins in ancient Greece. In classical Greek tragedies, hubris is often a fatal shortcoming that brings about the tragic hero's eventual fall.

I have seen many great people develop and nurture their hubris from seed to sapling to tree, especially when success, power or fame knocks enthusiastically at their door. Hubris can cloud and fog your judgment, placing you at the edge of the cliff surrounded by hubristic fog, unaware of the imminent fall that awaits.

Reflection: When Marcus Aurelius became Emperor of Rome, he was deeply concerned the power he now yielded would corrupt his virtues. He instructed a servant that accompanied him daily: "Every time a citizen bows a knee before me or calls out with praise, whisper in my ear – *you're only a man, you're only a man.*" Marcus Aurelius knew of the dangers of hubris and the fall that inevitably precursors its appearance. We are all susceptible to such traps that can befall us.

CHAPTER 54

It Is What It Is

"The best answer to anger is silence."
– Marcus Aurelius

My favourite Spanish phrase is: "es lo que es", which means 'it is what it is'.

Such a simple use of words, but as you may have already noticed while reading this book, some of the most profound statements are beautifully simple. Many of the models we explore within these pages connect at some level, sometimes in an undeniable context. At other times the connections are more vaporous, but connected nonetheless.

In this case, we can overlap Covey's *Circle of Concern* by asking the internal question; "Can I change or influence this?" If the answer is no, then the event whatever it may be falls neatly in the "es lo que es" category.

The ability to exercise indifference to the things that make no difference is a foundational skill of the Stoic philosophers and one we have explored within previous chapters.

Perhaps humans have an insatiable curiosity to get involved with events going on around us, even when they perhaps do not concern or affect us. This may be a contributing factor to the incredible collective evolution of our species. However, there is a trap embedded within this curiosity that kills cats and ensnares us within situations we cannot influence meaningfully. There is a particular connection we bind to when observing events. This binding connection can be challenging to sever once we're emotionally invested, bound by the psychological glues we call pride and judgement.

Do you have the ability to let things 'be' or do you get drawn into events you cannot control? Can you exercise the power of intentional disconnection from the circumstances that you have no control over?

Sometimes the attachment glue that bonds us to these events is strong, and the energy needed to sever them is considerable. However, the energy required to abandon a sinking ship is also significant, and we would not consider apathy in such situations. If you cannot change or affect the outcome, it is now a sinking ship that should you remain bound to, will inevitably take you to the bottom, one way or another.

Reflection: Many philosophers throughout history have advocated the merits of practising indifference, merely allowing that which does not matter or cannot be adjusted to pass by without unnecessary interference. Like with many elements of personal evolution, the start point of this pursuit is self-awareness; you cannot change what you have not acknowledged. Once you're aware of this, the next stage is to consciously create different neural pathways that lead to different choices.

As The Beatles famously sang: "*Let it be, let it be.*"

CHAPTER 55

Nuclear Waste

"Happiness is an absence of sufferings and anxiety."
– *Epicurus*

Imagine you have a metal drum which is full of nuclear waste, and the drum is sealed tight with little chance of the nuclear waste escaping. The problem remains you have no way to process the waste safely and do not want to keep it around in plain sight because of the danger contained within the drum. Therefore, the board members, executives, and decision makers call a meeting to decide the best course of action for the safe removal of the waste. In the meeting, various ideas are tabled and discussed. Finally, the executive committee decides the best course of action is to bury the drum at the bottom of the deep sea, many miles away from any country. The following day the drum is taken far out to sea by ship and, using remote underwater vehicles, buried at the bottom. Out of sight, out of mind.

Many years later, well past the tenure of the decision makers, the problem 'resurfaces' when the sealing around the metal drums starts corroding and consequently leaking radioactive waste into the ocean. Dead marine life starts washing up on the local beaches, and the natural habitat under the waves begins dying without explanation. Because the drum was buried such a long time ago, the newly elected politicians have no idea of the cause, and the executives of today are now presented with an entirely new challenge to solve.

One of the things I have noticed about humans is they sometimes can't, or don't want to, process events in their mind. The most common preference is to bury the event deep in the farthest recesses of their subconscious – the 'out of sight, out of mind' general solution. Problems may manifest many years later when these buried events begin to affect the person day-to-day, developing in several ways, including suffering physical and mental illness.

Now, I should emphasise at this juncture that I am not a psychologist nor therapist. My experience and training have been exclusively within coaching, although at times these overlapping demarcation lines are somewhat blurred between the various disciplines.

For me, I often turn to hypnosis when working with my clients. It's an approach I find to be at times breath-takingly effective. Over many years of studying and practising hypnosis, I have found it an uncommonly effective method of working my clients' 'unconscious' minds. Utilising hypnosis and working with a client's unconscious mind does not rely on conscious awareness of the problem's causation. My experience is often that this is entirely refreshing for my client because it alleviates the pressure to understand or 'figure out' what is happening, or why.

The responsibility to solve the presenting issue is, therefore, unburdened from the client.

I have incorporated hypnosis within my professional coaching for over ten years and have been continuously amazed by the results that can occur while using it. It is not a magic bullet, nor a panacea that solves everything. It is, however, superbly effective and something I urge all to try – even just to experience the state without a discernible purpose or reason.

Reflection: The accessing of different states of consciousness has been used for thousands of years, dating as far back as the start of recorded history with the ancient Egyptian priest, Imhotep (made famous by the Hollywood film *The Mummy*). You have already been hypnotised, probably without realising it, when watching a fantastic film, or perhaps when you drive your car and cannot recollect 'consciously' the journey. There are many books on hypnosis, which you can explore; these will be recognised in the bibliography at the end of the book.

CHAPTER 56

The Many Angles of Perspective – Three Stone Masons

"Everything we hear is an opinion, not a fact. Everything we see is a perspective, not the truth."
– Marcus Aurelius

During the late 16th century, work began on a cathedral in central Europe. The completion of such a monumental task in those times took many decades, even perhaps over a century. Assigned to the task was a clerk of the works whose job it was to ensure the necessary work standards were upheld; this weighty responsibility fell to one of the holiest monks. On the first day of his appointment, the clerk decided to visit three stonemasons to ascertain their perspective on their roles and how they saw the cathedral developing.

On visiting the first stonemason, the clerk of the works asked; "Tell me of the work you undertake and what it means to you."

The first stonemason replied; "I sit here on my stool each day, the block in front of me measures one metre, by one metre, by half a metre. Day after day, I repeat the same action. The work is tough and the weather unforgiving, my hands are worn and calloused, and I work with the knowledge that I shall never see the fruits of my labour, for this cathedral will not be finished till long after I am no longer of this earth. I work to provide for my family and to ensure we have food and shelter."

The clerk then approached the second stonemason and once more asked; "Tell me of the work you undertake, and its meaning to you."

The second stonemason replied, "I sit here on my stool each day, the block in front of me measures one metre, by one metre, by half a metre. Each day I am grateful for the opportunity to work. The work is indeed challenging, yet also rewarding. I work hard each day, and I am content that my work will contribute to this grand project, and that my children may be educated, so they do not need to undertake such relentless manual labour in their lives."

Finally, the clerk approached the third stonemason and again asked; "Tell me of the work you undertake, and its meaning to you."

The third stonemason replied, "I sit here on my stool each day, the block in front of me measures one metre, by one metre, by half a metre. Each day I feel truly blessed for the opportunity to contribute to this magnificent cathedral, and with each strike of my chisel, I can feel God's support and love. I work here day after day in the warming knowledge that I am contributing to something that will stand for many thousands of years. Although I may never see the completion with my eyes, I can see it now with my mind as clear as you stand beside me. My heart is full of gratitude, and no matter the weather, I savour each precious moment and feel blessed for the opportunity to put to work my craft. I can only pray that my children will also find a purpose worthy of the devotion of their life."

The clerk of the works resigned his post and apprenticed himself to the third stonemason.

Reflection: You can change the way you feel about anything by changing your perspective and modifying the language you choose to represent the event. The words you choose to describe the events of your life determine your feelings attributed to the event itself. Consider today which words you select to describe events in conversation, and where possible, improve your linguistic descriptions to change your internal perceptions.

Credit: The Magic of the Metaphor – Nick Owen

CHAPTER 57

Cause > Effect

"Chance is a word void of sense; nothing can exist without a cause."
– ***Voltaire***

Consider for a moment and fully connect with Voltaire's words above.

Also, consider the position you find yourself in right now, reading this chapter. How much of the life you find yourself presented with is because of chance and how much by design?

In nature, very few things are black or white; nature does not concern itself with the binary language of computers. Nature (Gaia) is analogue; it is not black or white, one or zero. It is, in fact, every perceivable colour and shade and perhaps many more outside our human perception. The vast majority of the models I use also reside in the analogue world of nature. There are occasional exceptions to the rule, however.

'Cause and Effect' is an example of a binary model. You are either on the 'Cause' side of the equation or the 'Effect'; there is no central ground to occupy. On the 'Effect' side of the equation, you have reasons (and sometimes excuses) for why you're not getting what you want, being who you want to be, or doing what you want to do. On the 'Cause' side of the equation, you only have your results. Whether they are the results you want, or not, is inconsequential – they are just your results.

My fiancée was diagnosed with a rare and incurable type of leukaemia called Chronic Myeloid Leukaemia (CML) 7 years ago. Ruth is a kind, thoughtful and incredibly caring person; everyone who meets her falls in love with her effervescent personality and selfless nature. Why should she deserve this chance disease caused by a mutated chromosome called the 'Philadelphia Chromosome'? The whole thing stinks of unfairness, a cosmic role of medical chance like a twisted lottery she never entered and even less wanted to win.

She did not deserve it, but the (harsh) truth is she does have it, and for a long time she struggled to come to terms with the reality of the situation, asking the existential question: "Why me?"

The defining moment that enabled her to control the situation was when she reversed this question and asked the inverse: "Why not me?"

Why shouldn't it be her? If it is to be this grand roll of nature's chance, why should someone else have to bear it and not her? Maybe if the dice rolled again, it might be her sister, friend, mother or even a poor child on the other side of the world who has no access to the marvellous treatment afforded to her by our NHS. Adopting this mindset allows her to move from the 'Effect' side of the equation to the 'Cause', so she takes ownership of the reality dealt to her by chance. She cannot control having this disease and she cannot control the cure, but she can have absolute control of her reaction to the situation. Now, I am not for one second implying this positional switch is easy. For Ruth, she had to work hard to move from one side to the other. Life will at times place you on the 'Effect' side without reason or whether you deserve it. Life can be a bitch as the saying goes, but you can choose your reaction to the hands chance deals.

As Viktor Frankl says in his seminal book *Man's Search for Meaning*: "When we are no longer able to change our situation, we are challenged to change ourselves."

Reflection: Although there may very well be randomness to the hands we are dealt in life, there is certainly nothing random about our reactions – ask any poker player this. You may not always get dealt the hand which you desire, but you can make the most of the cards in your hand.

CHAPTER 58

The Reality You Participate In

"Reality is created by the mind; we can change our reality by changing our mind."
– Parmenides

Parmenides holds a special place for me amongst the Greek philosophers of antiquity. By the time a youthful Socrates met Parmenides, he was an ageing man. This did not prevent Parmenides from greatly influencing the rapidly developing Socrates. Parmenides was a maverick philosopher and ran against the grain of many of his philosophical peers as they tried, and mostly failed, to comprehend what the elementary substance of reality was. Some philosophers believed reality to comprise of various combinations of the four essential elements: fire, earth, water, and air. Another of Socrates' teachers, Anaxagoras, believed that reality was created from an infinite number of particles or seeds, called 'spermata' which combine to create everything in the universe. Parmenides did not concern himself with such thinking, for he believed reality was an illusion, projected onto men's minds to occupy them through abstract boredom of objective reality.

It has been suggested that the Hollywood blockbuster film series *The Matrix* uses much of Parmenides' philosophical ideas. Even the concept of a 'paradox' has its early origins alongside these ideas. Para meaning 'contrary to' and Doxa, which means 'appearances', so many of Parmenides' ideas are 'contrary to appearances' or paradoxical.

Like Stoicism and Greek Philosophy, in general, there is much we can learn in our modern world from these great thinkers' ideas. Many people believe we cannot influence or control subjective reality, but of course we absolutely can, if we carefully think about it.

As Confucius once said; "*The man who thinks he can and the man who thinks he can't are both right.*" (Henry Ford later famously updated this quote.)

Like many times already within these pages, I am not claiming that thinking happy thoughts will manifest all your wants and desires into reality. I think the internet is already oversubscribed with such snake oil sellers preying on people's hopes and desires to instantly improve their situation, whatever that may be. What I am advocating here is the pursuit of controlling your inner world to transfer the influence to the outer world. The methodology of this lies in the daily application of the habits and behaviours described within these pages.

Cultivating your thinking takes time, and some days you'll nail it, others you won't. Humanities' greatest mistake in understanding the development of the conscious mind is to believe it is an episodic event, represented by attending a course or reading a book, instead of the continuous, unending, daily commitment to the pursuit of excellence. I have observed that most people only examine their minds at times of crisis; by this time, the horse has very much bolted from the stables. Continuous small commitments, undertaken each day, will always supersede intense, concentrated periods of focus and energy, especially after years of inactivity.

Reflection: Consider the work you undertake to improve your mindset to be a daily activity. Small behaviours repeated can lay the path to extraordinary results over time. The mind should be treated like all other muscles of the body – nourished well and worked out vigorously.

If you change the way you think, you will change your perception, and changing your perception will create new beliefs. New beliefs lead to different results.

CHAPTER 59

Moderate Your Moderation

"It is the part of a wise man to resist pleasures,
but of a foolish man to be a slave to them."
*– **Epictetus***

It is often thought one of the principles of Stoicism is the denial of humanistic pleasure. Because of this, Stoicism and Epicureanism are often pitted against each other as opposing philosophies and tend to create two distinct camps of followers. Like most things in life, it is not as easy as separating these two philosophies with a clear demarcation line. Both of these schools of philosophy flourished in the 3rd century BC in Athens, and there is value to be found in the principles of each of them.

In his statement above does the great Stoic, Epictetus, mean that we should have no pleasure, or does he mean we should not allow pleasures to enslave us?

There are certainly many differences between the two opposing philosophies, the principal difference being:

Epicureanism: The goal of life is to seek pleasure out and enjoy friends and learning, which leads to happiness.

Stoicism: The purpose of life is happiness, which is achieved by virtue, living according to the dictates of reason, ethical and philosophical training, self-reflection, careful judgement, and inner calm.

Both of these seem agreeable to me, and perhaps we can benefit from both pursuits? Also, there appears to be a central overlap insomuch as both point in the direction of happiness, which is subjective by its very nature.

Looking toward the future, our current enslavement to mobile phones has set us on a potentially perilous path. How often is your first action when waking up to check your phone? Perhaps you take your phone to the bathroom to 'pass the time' while attending business? If you lean too far toward the concept of Epicureanism, then perhaps the traps of modern living are set all around to snare and entangle. If, however, you were to lean too far towards Stoicism, maybe much of the enjoyment of engaging in the pleasures of modernity might be lost. It seems such a delicate balance.

As so often in the challenges we face, there is value in adopting and embracing both concepts into your life. Enjoy pleasure, but do not allow it to become your master, for then you become its slave. Perhaps start with your phone; this can be achieved by resisting the temptation to pick your phone up continually. Perhaps even place it in a separate room when you're enjoying the company of someone special, so they don't feel as though they're sharing your attention with the digital world.

Reflection: The wisdom of antiquity is as relevant today as it was thousands of years ago. We have evolved our environment exponentially in the time that has elapsed between Greece's ancient philosophers and the modern human holding a smart phone connected to the web. Although we have taken monumental strides in this short period of evolution, we should be mindful that our nervous system, and much of our biology, remains relatively unchanged.

CHAPTER 60

When the Going Gets Tough

"Prosperity is no just scale; adversity is the only balance to weigh friends."
– Plutarch

When Spartan warriors fought, they would rely on the man each side of them for their protection, and this tactical formation was called a Phalanx. In the Phalanx, the shields would overlap each other, creating a co-dependency of trust. Every Spartan protected with his shield, not only himself but also the man to his left, the weakest part of the Phalanx being the exposed right flank. It was considered dishonourable to lose a shield in any circumstance with the famous phrase spoken by Queen Gorgo to King Leonidas in the Hollywood film *300*: "Come back with your shield or on it."

Trust played a pivotal role in successfully adopting this formation, and the Phalanx is only ever as strong as its weakest point. Every man relied on the man next to him and trusted that man with their life.

Thankfully, we don't often need to go to war with our shields, swords, and spears in hand today. When venturing to work, our final farewells are not words such as; "Come home either with your shield or on it", but we do still rely on the person next to us from time to time.

As we rapidly ascend into the ever-increasing pace of the digital age, we need more than ever to fortify the human relationships closest to us. Our physical shield with the Spartan emblem has been replaced with our cognitive shield – our mind – but it is perhaps a more critical shield than we have ever needed in history. I am constantly dismayed by the rising statistics of mental health issues in this 'evolved' and 'civilised' world we've created. It can, at times, seem like a real pandemic, largely going by unspoken, unnoticed and unchecked. This general dismay is exacerbated by personal experiences of losing friends to mental health issues, which I wholly believe were avoidable.

We must take back responsibility for our shields and then start interlocking for a Phalanx formation of protection.

How on earth do we do this though? What are the steps to taking control of your shield?

Firstly, it is about understanding and applying some of the ideas, concepts, and principles we have explored within these pages. Daily habits return tremendous rewards when applied with consistency and commitment. Doing the small things daily leads to the most remarkable improvement over time, yet this spawns the obvious question – why aren't we doing them already then? Secondly, it is about cultivating those relationships that mean the most, not the superficial Twitter followers, or barely connected Facebook friends, but the people who matter in your life. In all honesty, the people in your Phalanx should number less than ten and contain only those people with whom you have a strong bond. Work on these connections and spend time cultivating the bonds that exist between you in the knowledge that there may be a time when they're your person on the left, or you theirs.

The famous Roman Dictator Perpetuo, Julius Caesar, once said, *"As a rule, what is out of sight disturbs men's minds more seriously than what they see."*

Reflection: Who are the people in your life that matter? Who is in your close friend group? Establish this clearly, then examine the strength of the connection between these friends. Place time and energy in fortifying these links in the knowledge that one day you may find yourself in need of vital support from someone else's shield. It won't be your Twitter followers on the field of battle, I can assure you of this.

CHAPTER 61

If You're Not Living On The Edge, You're Taking Up Too Much Room

---

"The greater the difficulty, the more glory in surmounting it."
*– **Epicurus***

Humans, as a collective generalisation, are not natural risk-takers. We are evolutionarily hardwired to move away from potential danger. Our adventurous and curious ancestors' lineage might have struggled to continue replicating against the more conservative of the tribe.

I remember perfectly the visceral feeling of terror in the pit of my stomach as I sat on the train to Commando Training Centre Royal Marines (CTCRM) Lympstone in October 1998. I was travelling to undertake my training to become a Royal Marine Commando. The feeling of complete helplessness mixed with the impending uncertainty that shrouded my immediate future gnawed away at my stomach. I can only compare it to the first time you get into trouble as a child and are sent to wait outside the headmaster's office. The uncertainty of not knowing what horror was to come, while concurrently having the absolute certainty that whatever was going to happen was about to happen, and there was no escaping this destiny. There were so many unknowns on that train: I didn't know who my training team would be, nor any of the recruits, and I wasn't sure when I would eat next, although my appetite was already absent.

I was uncertain of everything, except two things: whatever was going to happen, it was going to happen (soon), and I was terrified to my core. Uncertainty terrifies humans and at its extreme can leave us incapacitated, unable to think or even comprehend the actions needed to take us away from the situation we may have found ourselves in. Away from this extremity, it prevents us from doing 'stuff' we should be doing because of fear.

Fear is, without doubt, the captor, guard and prison warden of our dreams and ambitions. Almost certainly the things you fear have prevented you from committing to the pursuit of your desires. It's the reason most people settle into a job they are adequately happy with, or into a life which is barely comparable with their dreams of childhood, yet they lack the necessary courage to pursue their real dreams.

Fear, fear, fear!

Letting go of this fear is for many of my clients their highest priority, although often it is not why they initially seek out the support of a coach. Epicurus understood the debilitating effect of fear. Most of his philosophical approach was to enable himself to become free from 'aponia' (the absence of physical pain) and 'ataraxia' (the absence of mental disturbance). In summary, freedom of the mind and body. The first step to attaining such a worthy prize is to confront fear and learn that it is rarely as scary in reality as it is in your imagination.

Although CTCRM Lympstone was without exception the most significant challenge I have faced, both physically and mentally, it was not, and could not, be as terrible as my imagination envisaged. I genuinely believe that anyone who has the tenacity and drive can complete Royal Marine Commando training. That is by no means devaluing the task at hand and fit, well-disciplined, and ambitious potential Royal Marine Commandos fall by the wayside every day. Some do not even pass the interviews. My point is that it is nearly entirely a matter of the mind, rather than limitations of the body.

Reflection: We all experience fear. It is what has kept you alive to this point, and without it, you will most likely create an early appointment with your maker. Fear that prevents you from doing something you desire is debilitatingly different. This fear will cripple your ambitions, castrating your dreams. This fear should be examined, reflected on, and dismantled. The only thing to fear is fear itself, after all.

CHAPTER 62

Paying Attention – The Boy and The Spoon

"The purpose of life is the investigation of the Sun, the Moon and the Heavens."

– Anaxagoras

A young boy awoke one morning with a burning question at the forefront of his mind. The boy marched buoyantly into the family kitchen, boldly asking his father without breaking stride; "Father, what is the meaning of life?"

The father, dumbfounded by this profoundly philosophical question, responded in the way fathers sometimes do; "That's a great question, son, perhaps ask your mother." The curious boy dutifully took his question to his mother; "Mother, what is the meaning of life?"

"Fantastic question, my son" she replied thoughtfully, "perhaps you might ask the wise teacher who lives high in the hills. You'll have to wait until summer to ascend the mountain safely, my son."

The young boy waited patiently as winter drew in. Eventually, winter gave way to spring and finally, the longer, warmer days of summer emerged. The young boy had studied the route and knew he would need to hike for hour upon hour, he knew he would need to climb what seemed to be a never-ending ascent of the mountain. Nonetheless he set about his task.

Eventually, the young boy arrived at the monastery on top of the mountain where the wise teacher lived. People travelled from all kingdoms to ask only one question per person. There were young people and older people, lawmakers and criminals, rich people and poor, and everything in between. All who came, regardless of wealth or status, were only granted one question each.

Hours passed as the boy waited patiently in line before his time finally arrived to ask his only question. He strolled toward where the wise teacher sat and asked his single question; "Wise teacher, what is the meaning of life?"

The teacher looked intently into the eyes of the boy before allowing a nearly imperceptible smile.

"My boy, I shall need some time to think over this great question. In the meantime, take some time to visit my home and wonder at its beauty. Take off your shoes, for it is the custom in this land, and in doing so, feel the smooth coolness of the mosaic floors under your bare feet. Take time to look and appreciate the fine hanging tapestries in my halls, noticing the combinations of stunning colours and the artist's rich detail. Allow your ears to be filled with my musicians' glorious sounds in the gardens, and they will delight and enchant your soul. While in the gardens also do not miss my orchards for the sweet aromas will arrest your senses and transport you to a land of forgotten memories. Finally, be certain to visit my kitchens and taste the foods my chefs prepare, their produce and expert preparation will excite your tastes beyond comprehension."

As the boy was about to leave, the wise teacher stopped him, taking from his pocket a small spoon and bottle of oil; he then placed two tiny drops of oil onto the spoon.

"Just one final thing before you go, take this spoon and take care for under no circumstances should you spill these two special drops. Come back in two hours, and I will answer your question."

Precisely two hours passed, and the boy returned to the chamber of the wise teacher. The teacher asked; "And did you feel the smooth texture of the floors, see the colourful tapestries, inhale the eloquent aromas from my gardens, taste the beautiful food prepared by my chefs, and hear the sweet sounds of my musicians?"

The little boy shook his head and said, "No. I did none of these things, but look, wise teacher, I still have the two drops of oil on my spoon you requested I take care of!"

The wise teacher paused for a moment and looked deep into the eyes of the young boy and then said; "My son, never trust anyone whose house you do not know. Go back again and take the time to notice everything there is to notice, and truly appreciate everything there is to appreciate. Use all of your senses and experience the wonder of all the elements I have described. Once you have truly experienced my house and all it has to offer, return again with the spoon and the two drops of oil and I will answer your question."

The boy revisited all the rooms in the wise teacher's house, using all of his senses to experience the wonder in each area as the teacher had requested. When he returned to the teacher's chamber, he was ecstatic and bursting with joy and energy.

Full of wonder and amazement, he spoke enthusiastically, "Oh, it's wonderful, wise teacher! I saw tapestries with their stunning colours and detail. I heard the music of the finest musicians and danced freely. I walked on the cool floors and tried all of the mouth-watering dishes. I also smelled the sweet aromas of all the flowers in the gardens and orchards. Finally, I felt the smooth cold mosaics underneath my feet. Everything was completely wonderful!"

"It is indeed wonderful," replied the wise teacher. "May I also enquire to the fate of the drops of oil on your journey?"

When the boy looked down at the spoon, he realised he had dropped the oil in his excitement.

'And this, my precious boy, is the meaning of life," the wise teacher said quietly. "You see, it is quite simple: to absorb the world around, you must use all of your senses to appreciate the wonder of all there is to experience. Each of your senses is a priceless gift that should be embraced to its fullest potential. Only once this is mastered will you realise the whole world is there to serve you and reach your goals. However, you should always pay attention to the small details around you at the same time as this. While being amazed by what the world has to offer, you should always be aware of the small drops in your possession."

Reflection: It's easy at times to become *tunnel* visioned in life focussing our attention on what is directly infront of us. Conversely it is also easy to be overwhelmed by the entire universe and the realisation of our insignificance upon this great backdrop. Paying attention to and having awareness of both isn't easy simultaneously, but nonetheless a worthy philosophical pursuit.

Original source: *Paolo Coelho, The Alchemist*

Secondary source: *Nick Owen, The Magic of Metaphor*

CHAPTER 63

Tie Yourself To The Mast If You Want To Succeed

"I came, I saw, I conquered."
– Julius Caesar

Homer's *The Odyssey* is recognised as one of the oldest examples of literature known today alongside his other masterpiece *The Iliad*. These are some of the few pieces that survived the great fire of the Alexandria Library in 48 BC, a day in which an untold amount of ancient wisdom was lost forever. In *The Odyssey*, Homer recounts the ten-year journey Odysseus (later named Ulysses by the Romans) undertook to return from the Trojan war. During this epic ten-year adventure, Ulysses was beset by all manner of challenges and creatures, mortal and God. One encounter was with the cyclops who were giant shepherds with one eye on their central forehead. Ulysses would blind Polyphemus the cyclops when rescuing his men from Polyphemus' cave. Unfortunately, Ulysses had not realised that Polyphemus was also the son of Poseidon, the Sea God. In retaliation for his son being blinded, Poseidon relentlessly ravaged Ulysses back to the shores of Ithaca.

One of the most famous tales from Ulysses' adventures was his encounter with the sirens. The sirens were mystical creatures that sang songs so beautiful and enchanting that sailors would drown themselves, or shipwreck their vessels, to join the sirens on the beach. It was believed the sirens sang of the greatest desires of the listener. For Ulysses, this was his wife, Penelope, his son, Telemachus, as well as unlimited knowledge.

Ulysses desperately wanted to hear the song, but did not want to die in the process. Also, he was warned of the perils of the sirens by the enchanting Circes who had bewitched his men on a previous adventure, turning them to animals before Ulysses saved them with the help of the messenger God, Hermes. To be able to hear the song without drowning himself or his men, Ulysses instructed his crew to fill their ears with bees' wax and tie him tightly to the ship's mast. He also gave orders to his crew that in no eventuality should they untie him from the mast until they were well clear of the song of the sirens. Until then, they were to hold their course resolutely until the task was complete. Because of this, Ulysses became the only living man to hear the sirens' song and live to tell the tale.

In our modern world, there is a concept called a 'Ulysses Contract'. This contract is a modern version of Ulysses' strategy to complete his Odyssey task of hearing the sirens' song and not dying. Imagine my new year goal is to go to the gym three times per week. There may be mornings when I am tired or lack the motivation, or perhaps I have forgotten to organise my gym bag for whatever reason. There will always be reasons not to do things that are tiresome and require effort. However, if I enter into a 'Ulysses Contract' with a friend, there is more likelihood of me staying true to my course, regardless of the challenges and pitfalls that await. The contract works because if we both agree to meet each other and hold each other accountable, then when my partner or I lack motivation, we will still turn up to not let the other down. We are both tied to the mast using the rope of pride, and in doing so, our course is now set together.

Reflection: Consider the elements of your life that take resolve and motivation to follow through to completion, then ask yourself the question; "How can I apply a Ulysses Contract to this to ensure I follow it through to completion?" Who can you bind yourself to for mutual accountability to ensure you both stay on course and finish what you start?

CHAPTER 64

Who Governs Your Head?

"There are many worlds and many systems of universes existing all at the same time, all of them perishable."
– Anaximander

Anaximander was a fascinating Greek philosopher who lived in the pre-Socratic time of the 6th century BC. Although referred to as one of the pre-Socratic Greek philosophers, he was actually from Miletus, or Turkey as it would later be known. Often credited as the first scientist and wonderfully brought to life by Carlo Rovelli in his magnificent book 'The First Scientist: Anaximander and his Legacy'.

Anaximander was the pupil of Thales in the Milesian School of Philosophy and eventually succeeded Thales as Master of the School. Later he influenced prominent philosophers such as Anaximenes and Pythagoras. Anaximander is also attributed as the father of astronomy as he was the first celestial thinker to develop cosmology using mathematical proportions to map the heavens.

An analogy is often made between the universe that occupies the space above our head, and the mind that occupies the space under our skull. Both are expansive, both have trillions of connections, and both have piqued the curiosity of man since the dawn of time. Our species still has much to learn about our consciousness; in some ways, we know more about the universe 'above' our head than we do the universe 'within' it.

What is consciousness? Where does it come from, and how did it evolve? How are our memories stored unconsciously and consciously retrieved at will? These are some of the questions that remain at the vanguard of neuroscience.

Your brain is actually a team of individual brains woven together in the womb of your mother. Each has a different agenda and at times these agendas can, and do, oppose each other. We could use an analogy to understand better that our brains are not necessarily a single unit. Consider this as a concept: the House of Commons comprises 650 elected officials known as 'Members of Parliament' (MPs). These MPs belong to political parties, and currently, ten parties have representation in the House, with one independent and the Speaker of the House. Some parties, such as the Conservative and Labour parties, are much larger with 365 and 200 current MPs, respectively. The other parties range from forty-seven seats for the Scottish Nationalist Party (SNP), down to only one seat held by the Green Party.

In many ways, your mind is a composition of competing factions with often opposing beliefs, agendas and arguments but, most importantly, all doing what they think to be 'right' for the greater good. Your brain is evidentially the seat of decision making for the rest of your body. The Houses of Parliament perform a similar decisional responsibility for the wider country. All being well, we hope that our logical human brain, represented by the frontal cortex, has the majority of votes and can perform the executive decision maker's role. More emotionally driven brains can often combine and defeat the logical brain and take over the executive decision-making process. Rather than relying on logic for our decisions, we are sometimes fuelled by emotion. This 'emotional' thinking can result in rash choices often regretted by the logical brain at a later date. Perhaps this happens more than we care to admit to ourselves?

Reflection: Diplomacy is often the key to understanding the positions of all the competing factions, even the unruly minority which shouts the loudest. Paying close attention to 'what' you're thinking and 'when', as well as the outcome of certain repetitive thinking, will help you gain control of your emotional brain and lead you to make better decisions. Yet, each part of your thought process has validity. To a certain extent, whether you agree with it or not, it will have a positive intention at some level – just like all the competing elements of Parliament. To get the most from your thinking, understand the wants and needs and get to know all of the parties in play; that is the key to successful brain politics.

CHAPTER 65

Comfort - Stretch - Panic

"It is not the critic who counts; not the man who points out how the strong man stumbles, or where the doer of deeds could have done better. The credit belongs to the man who is actually in the arena, whose face is marred by the dust and sweat and blood; who knows great enthusiasms, the great devotions; who spends himself in a worthy cause; who at best knows in the end the triumph of high achievement, and who at the worst, if he fails, at least fails while daring greatly, so that his place shall never be with those cold and timid souls who neither know victory nor defeat."

– Theodore Roosevelt

One of my favourite learning models is also one of the simplest; strange how simplicity is often simultaneously beautiful. I learned this model while coaching in the Royal Air Force (RAF) and have since used it for many clients. Specifically, my job in the RAF was known as an Adventure Training Instructor (ATI). Essentially, my role was to utilise the great outdoors to develop our personnel using a combination of adventurous activities with performance coaching. Typically, we would use mountaineering, climbing, kayaking and canoeing, skiing and ski touring etc. However, these activities only told part of the story as the essential work was done before the morning's activity and on return late in the afternoon. In these sessions, we would review the day using developmental models to help the personnel comprehend and absorb what they had learned from the day. Often, we would intentionally place them in perceived fear while managing their safety. In these situations, the airmen and women would expand their limitations through experience.

The Comfort / Stretch / Panic model was one of my favourites to help the young servicemen and women learn to manage their fear. Fear harms far fewer people than compliancy, in my experience, but being frozen when a critical decision is needed can be catastrophic! We need our soldiers, sailors and airmen to understand and accept fear as part of their developmental journey. Being brave is never about defeating fear insomuch as it's about learning to accept fear and still make decisions and take action regardless. We've already established in early chapters that as humans, we inherently want to stay within our comfort bubbles. It is safe and known there, and our limbic emotional brain does not like danger in any context, whether actual or perceived. However, we also know that if we can step outside of our 'Comfort' zone and into the 'Stretch' zone, feeling fear and nervousness, we are rewarded with an immense feeling of self-pride and satisfaction as well as an expansion of our self-belief.

Have you ever done a charity abseil or perhaps even a sky-dive? How did you feel after completion? This expansion of self-belief changes our comfort and stretch zones, expanding the boundaries of both, similar to blowing air into a balloon. Although the balloon's physical properties remain the same, it expands, develops, and grows as more air is forced inside. There is a point though that if we were to blow too much air into the balloon, it would burst. This burst occurs when we go over the 'Stretch' boundary into the 'Panic' zone, placing too much duress on the balloon in the process. Where possible we would ideally sit just beneath this demarcation line constantly expanding our 'Stretch' zone while understanding that too much, too soon could burst the balloon completely.

Reflection: What can you do today to expand your 'Stretch' zone and grow? Have you always wanted to try something, but the fear of the activity outweighs the reward of completion? Why not use the 'Ulysses Contract' (Chapter 63) to bind yourself with a friend to complete the challenge? Pay attention to how you feel after you have completed the task and notice how your balloon will have stretched.

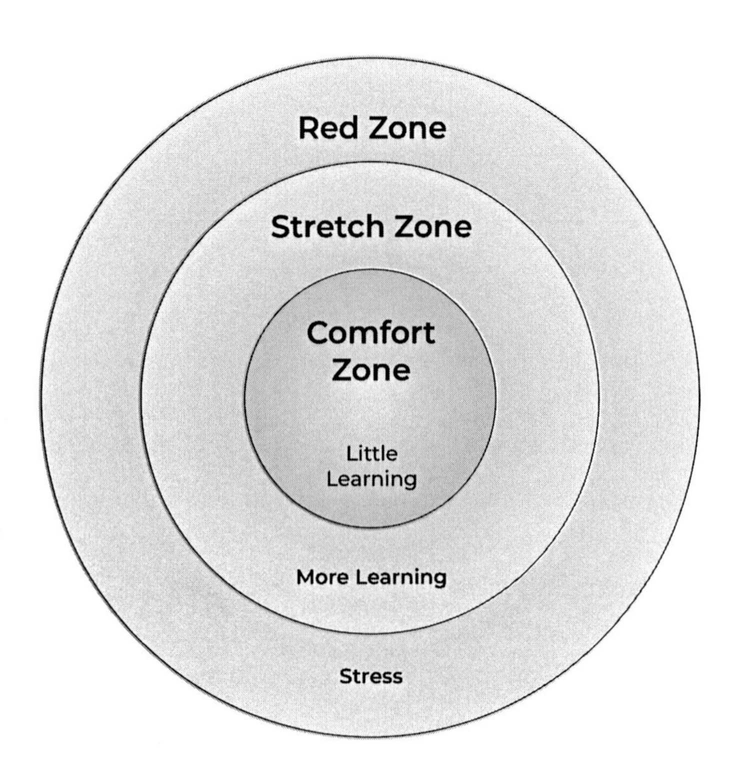
Red Zone
Stretch Zone
Comfort
Zone
Little
Learning
More Learning
Stress

CHAPTER 66

Timeless

"If all the insects were to disappear from earth, within 50 years all life on earth would end. If all human beings disappeared from the earth, within 50 years all forms of life would flourish."

– Jonas Salk

And people stayed home
And read books and listened
And rested and exercised
And made art and played
And learned new ways of being
And stopped
And listened deeper
Someone meditated
Someone prayed
Someone danced
Someone met their shadow
And people began to think differently
And people healed

And in the absence of people who lived in ignorant ways
Dangerous, meaningless and heartless,
Even the earth began to heal
And when the danger ended
And people found each other
Grieved for the dead people
And they made new choices
And dreamed of new visions
And created new ways of life
And healed the earth completely
Just as they were healed themselves.

Catherine (Kitty) O'Meara

This wonderful poem was written in 2020 by a retired schoolteacher to describe the world under Covid lockdown.

Where we find ourselves today is in the wake of this global event. Lives were prematurely lost, businesses went under, and marriages and families were placed under incredible strain; some survived, and some did not. But throughout this adversity, there were many, many examples of extraordinary courage and resilience.

But what does this poem say *to* you? What does it say *about* you? What does it say about us *collectively*? How many of the things the author describes in this poem did you participate in, or notice, during the Covid-19 pandemic?

Reflection: We often pray only in times of despair and appreciate what we have when we are about to lose them. The global pandemic shone an uncomfortable light on the fragility of our collective mental resilience. We will, I suspect, not fully understand the full repercussions from this event for many years to come. There will certainly be many positives to draw as well as many lessons hopefully learnt.

CHAPTER 67

Zeno of Citium

"Man conquers the world by conquering himself."
– Zeno of Citium

It seems peculiar that it should take me sixty-seven chapters to arrive at the philosopher who started Stoicism, especially as the philosophy has permeated many of the pages before this point.

Stoicism took its name from the place where Zeno started his lectures – the Stoa Piokile (Painted Colonnade). Influenced during the changing times of the post-Platonic and post-Aristotelian eras in Athens, Stoicism emerged as the forerunner of philosophical schools during the transitional Hellenistic Age. Zeno was influenced by many philosophers including Aristotle and Socrates (who had died about 100 years prior) and attended Plato's Academy to form Stoicism's philosophical skeleton. Zeno's direct teachers were Crates of Thebes, Stilpo the Megarian, and later Polemo.

Zeno was originally a wealthy Cypriot merchant who lost his fortune when his merchant ship was lost at sea. He was consoled by Crates of Thebes who taught him that material possessions were of no importance whatsoever to happiness. On hearing the news that all of his luggage and belongings had been lost at sea, Zeno was famously quoted as saying: *"Fortune bids me to be a less encumbered philosopher."*

One of the essential elements of Zeno's thinking was that the basis of human happiness was to live "in agreement with oneself". This statement was later replaced by "to live in agreement with nature". It is difficult to reconcile how far we've strayed from this path with our modern world of consumerism, excess, and reckless use of earth's natural resources. I have wondered what the ancient Greek philosophers would think if they were to be transferred by time machine to the world of 2021 – perhaps they would look at their own country's economic plight and wonder where on earth it all went wrong fiscally?

The second and third heads of the Stoic school, Cleanthes and Chrysippus, further enhanced Zeno's work. Over time, Stoicism became the dominant philosophy to the Roman republic under the times of emperors like Julius Caesar and Nero, then later Marcus Aurelius. The prominent Stoic philosopher, Seneca the Younger, was the long-time adviser and educator to Nero before falling out of favour with the emperor and subsequently being forced to commit suicide on Nero's orders.

One thing is certain about Zeno of Citium – his ideas and philosophy have stood the test of time, with Stoicism's concepts as relevant today as they were in the 3rd century BC, in Athens. Perhaps, this can be significantly attributed to some of the later Stoics such as Marcus Aurelius, Seneca and Epictetus? Regardless of this they all waked the path that Zeno first paved once shipwrecked in Athens.

Reflection: I urge you to adopt the ideas we've explored in previous chapters and examine your own life through philosophical principles. It matters not if you are rich or poor, the quality of your thoughts will decide the outcome of your happiness. You cannot expect to establish control of your life if you first cannot control your thoughts. Wherever you find yourself today, consider Zeno the wealthy Cypriot merchant; a man who lost all his possessions and concluded from the tragedy he was destined *"to be a less encumbered philosopher"*.

CHAPTER 68

Stoic Principle – Look Inside Yourself

"Every man thinks of changing the world, but
no man thinks of changing himself."
– Leo Tolstoy

The Story of The Littlest God

After the Battle of the Titans, the victorious Olympian Gods were celebrating their victory on Mount Olympus. After ten years of war, Cronus and the Titan Gods had been banished to Tartarus (the underworld), and it was now the time of Zeus and the Olympian Gods to rule.

The Olympians were celebrating their hard-fought victory with a lavish banquet. There was music, merriment and much wine consumed by the Gods. During the celebration, Poseidon, who was the Sea God, posed a question to the other immortals; "What is our greatest creation as Gods?"

All of the Gods hotly debated this question by the Sea God until Hades finally responded with the proclamation that the

Gods' most incredible creation was, in fact, the humans who walked the earth upright, similar to Gods themselves. The other Gods met this statement with universal agreement, and with as much backslapping and pompousness that is to be expected of divine beings.

Once the chorus of self-congratulating dissolved another question was again postulated by Poseidon.

"Well, if the humans are our best creation, what separates us from them?"

Silence fell, and the Gods turned and looked at each other in confusion before one of the smaller Gods pointed out. "Well, it's simply a case of resources. We, as Gods, have better resources than the humans who are limited below." Once again, the noise erupted as all of the Gods agreed that they indeed had better resources than the humans.

Then, the same God asked a question that shook the Gods and the mountain they stood on, "What if humans discover our divine resources?"

The mountainside erupted as the Gods set about the immediate debate of where to hide their resources. The first God, Prometheus, suggested hiding the resources on top of the highest mountain. However, it was quickly pointed out that humans would discover them because eventually, they would climb the highest mountains. The next God suggested hiding the divine resources in the deepest caves, but once again, it was agreed that humans explored the deepest caves. Finally, Aphrodite suggested placing them at the bottom of the deepest ocean. It was decided that humans cannot breathe underwater and were unable to reach the deepest ocean floors. But then one God pointed out that although they cannot breathe underwater, they were gifted the ability to invent and build and one day would create a contraption that would allow them to explore the deepest seas.

It was a problem that vexed all of the Olympian Gods. That was until the smallest God quietly spoke. This God, although petite in size, was one of the wisest Gods. Her name was Athena and all of the Gods listened intently. "It is simple; hide the resources inside the humans. They will look everywhere but there for our divine resources."

Reflection: We are more than we could ever imagine, but to discover our true capability we must search deep inside ourselves first. Adversity reveals our hidden potential, and we just need the courage and resilience to dig deep and go past our fears. This is the quest you undertake for your Agoge, to find out who you are and what you really can achieve.

CHAPTER 69

Plato's Cave

"Those who are able to see beyond the shadows and lies of their culture will never be understood let alone believed by the masses."

– Plato

Socrates was famed for writing very little of his own philosophy down. It was left to his brightest student, Plato, to record his many ideas. Because of this, it is sometimes difficult to discern which ideas were Socrates, and which were Plato's with a lead character called Socrates. However, we can be confident of Plato's own work, as unlike his teacher he was prolific with his writing.

One of Plato's most famous pieces of work is the Socratic dialogue *The Republic*. This was his concept of a utopian, just society built upon four virtues: wisdom, courage, moderation, and justice. You may notice these are not dissimilar to the four Stoic virtues. In Book VII of *The Republic*, Plato famously wrote about his Allegory of the Cave.

In the cave, prisoners are bound in the dark and can only observe the wall at the cave's back. Behind the prisoners is a fire that their captors use to cast shadows on the cave's back wall. Because the cave prisoners have never been outside, they know only of the shadows cast against the wall, which their captors create. They may observe the appearance of a fox, a bird, or other humans, but they are only watching illusions created by the fire projecting shadows onto the back of the cave.

Because the cave prisoners are not aware that anything exists outside the cave and can only observe the back of the cave and are not even aware the fire exists behind them, their 'reality' is the observable shadows cast against the wall.

The paradox begins when one of the prisoners is released from this bondage. At first, the newly freed prisoner might fear the captors removing his chains. He first notices the fire and perhaps sees in the distance there is a faint light at the hitherto unseen cave entrance. Suspiciously glancing around the cave for the first time, the prisoner is terrified to leave the back of the cave, and he needs dragging towards the light at the exit of the cave. Staggering towards the cave's mouth, his limbs feel odd and sights and sounds he's never before seen or heard begin to arrest his senses. Walking outside the cave for the first time, the released prisoner struggles to adjust to the blinding light after a life of darkness. As his eyes slowly re-adjust to the bright daylight, he now notices for the first-time real birds and foxes, as well as humans walking outside the cave in the light.

He now sees *reality*.

Does he go back inside the cave where it is safe? Is outside the cave reality, or is it inside? Should he return to free the other prisoners? If he did return to the cave, would they even believe his stories of the world outside the cave, his terrifying new reality?

Reflection: This can often be a challenge faced by people when they have a significant paradigm shift in their life. Perhaps they have a deeply religious experience and witness God for the first time. This monumental event triggers them to convert to the Church immediately and devote their life entirely to God. How do their friends and family then react to this new 'reality'?

This can also happen occasionally after attending personal development courses that can lead to paradigm shifts in a person's thinking. Out of these seismic experiences, it can sometimes be challenging to adequately explain these new ideas to friends and family who have known them for many years. Perhaps they are still in the cave, and no matter how much you explain the world outside, if they're just not ready to leave. You may have to accept it.

CHAPTER 70

The Coffee, The Egg & The Potato

"The most difficult thing to know in life is yourself."
– Thales of Miletus

Once upon a time, a daughter complained to her father that her life was miserable, and at times she didn't know how she was going to make it through life. She was fatigued from the battles and struggles that she seemed to face constantly. From her perspective, as soon as one problem was solved another appeared to challenge her once more.

Her father, who was a wise chef, took her into his kitchen as he often did to espouse wisdom. He proceeded to fill three pots with cold water then placed each one on the stove in front of his now perplexed daughter. As the three pots began their journey toward a rolling boil, he carefully placed one egg, one potato, and some coffee beans on the work bench. The daughter looked on, unsure of the reason behind her father's strange behaviour.

Once the pots reached a gentle boil, and without saying a word to his daughter, the father placed the egg into one pot, the potato in the next, and finally the coffee beans in the third. The daughter began to complain, impatiently wondering what the meaning was behind this seemingly unconnected task. The father gently smiled and encouraged his daughter to observe the three pots of water and their contents.

After twenty minutes, the father turned the stove off and placed the pots on the table. He took the potato and the egg out of their pots and put them in a bowl, then he took a ladle full of the coffee and poured it into a cup next to the bowl.

Turning to his daughter, the chef asked; "Daughter, what do you see in front of you?"

The daughter hastily replied; "A potato, an egg and some coffee, obviously!"

"Look closer," the chef replied. "Perhaps touch the potato."

The daughter indeed felt the potato and noted it was soft. The chef then asked to her break the egg, which the daughter duly complied with, and after pulling away the shell she recognised the egg was hard-boiled and firm. Finally, he asked her to take a sip from the cup of coffee; its rich aroma brought a smile to her face as she enjoyed coffee immensely.

"But Father, what does this mean?"

The chef then explained that the potato, egg and the coffee had all faced the same adversity – boiling water. The potato went in strong, hard and unrelenting, but in the water had become soft to touch. The egg was fragile with only a thin outer shell to protect the yolk inside but once it experienced the relentless heat from the water, it began to toughen and harden through the process. Finally, however, the coffee beans went in, and they were unique. After they were exposed to the same boiling water, they changed the water entirely and transformed it into something completely different.

The chef then turned to his daughter and asked, "Which of these represents you? When adversity knocks on your door, how do you respond? Are you like the potato, the egg or the coffee beans?"

Credit: www.businessballs.com

Reflection: Once again, I think Viktor Frankl can most eloquently summarise this: *"When we are no longer able to change a situation, we are challenged to change ourselves."*

CHAPTER 71

How To Measure The Circumference of Earth; 2000 Years Ago

"Mathematics reveals its secrets only to those who approach it with pure love, for its own beauty."
– Archimedes

Imagine I set you a task to complete, perhaps it is the most monumental problem to solve. The job is simple in the request, but gigantic in the undertaking. I want you to measure the earth's circumference with a one metre stick, and it's the year 240 BC.

Eratosthenes was the curator of the great library of antiquity, The Alexandria Library. He was often referred to as the 'Beta Philosopher', primarily because his academic interests spanned so many varying subjects from mathematics to poetry, botany to astrology, metaphysics to geography, and everything in between. It was safe to proclaim Eratosthenes was an incredible intellect. He began his studies in Athens, like many of the great philosophers, but was requested to go to Alexandria by the Egyptian ruler, Ptolemy III, to tutor his son, and Eratosthenes later became the curator of the library.

Within The Alexandria Library, Eratosthenes discovered a papyrus script that described a city south of Alexandria called Syene (now Aswan). On the summer solstice in Syene, according to the papyrus script, you could place a one metre stick into the ground, and it cast no shadow in any direction. However, when Eratosthenes attempted the same experiment in Alexandria, which was north of Syene, on the same day, he found the stick cast a shadow of 7°12' from the vertical.

With this basic knowledge, Eratosthenes knew that should he be able to measure Syene and Alexandria's distance, he could use relatively simple geometry to ascertain the earth's circumference. Greek philosophers had known since around 500 BC that the world was round and until Aristotle, it was hotly debated by various philosophers whether the earth orbited the sun, or vice versa. Eratosthenes' method for measuring the distance between Alexandria and Syene was to incorporate walkers who were trained to measure distances by taking regular strides. The distance ascertained was 5,000 Stadia, which works out at approximately 500 miles (or 800 km). With the distance between the two cities now known and the 7°12' difference from the shadows cast, he had enough data to work out one slice of the circle, effectively like a slice from a round pie.

He did this by using this simple division:

360 (degrees in circle) ÷ 7°12' (angle of shadow in) = 50

50 x 50,000 (distance in stadia) = 250,000 stadia / 25,000 miles / 40,250km

True circumference – 40,096km

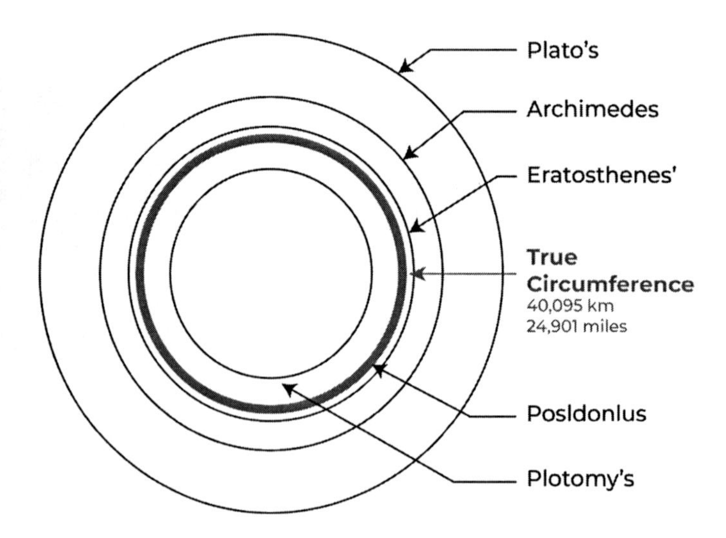

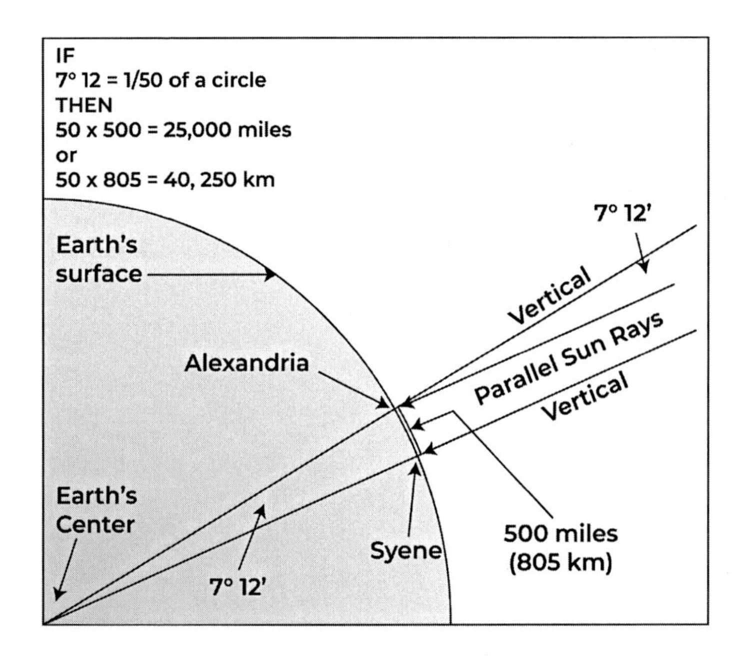

Reflection: Eratosthenes solved this almost unimaginable problem by applying simple mathematical principles. Often In life when we are first presented a complex problem to solve we immediately assume that the solution ought to be as complex as the presenting problem. This is not always the case. Sometimes taking a step back and observing and taking the time to think clearly can strip away to a simple solution.

CHAPTER 72

Your Google Brain

"He who has peace of mind disturbs neither himself nor another."
*– **Epicurus***

Have you ever noticed how your brain is a pattern-searching machine? Perhaps if I use an analogy followed by an example of what I am suggesting it might resonate with you?

Imagine for a moment you decide to upgrade your home sound system. After some research and comparing various products, you choose to purchase Sonos speakers through Amazon. While waiting for your new speakers to arrive, you carry on reading reviews and studying your imminent audio upgrade via various websites. Then the strangest thing starts to happen; suddenly across your digital devices, you begin noticing adverts for Sonos audio speakers. On Facebook and Instagram, as well as when you're browsing the Internet or watching videos on YouTube – these adverts keep popping up as if your computer knows what you want. Now, it's obvious what is happening here for most people – you've searched these items, so they're in your HTTP cookies, supposedly to improve your browsing experience on the internet but more often associated with re-target advertising.

Your brain works similarly through something called your 'Reticular Activating System' or simply your RAS.

You will most likely be familiar with when your RAS is working but perhaps not consciously aware of it. Can you remember the last car you purchased? I would imagine that before purchasing you might have researched some of the models and colours you were interested in, perhaps then narrowing the search down to a few dealerships which had the car you wanted in the colour you wanted, and at the price you were willing to pay? Finally, you committed to one of the dealers and placed the order for your car, but unfortunately, your dream car took a week or so to order and prepare. In the meantime, whilst driving around in your old vehicle, what started to happen? You started noticing the car you'd just bought, in the same colour, the same model, everywhere you travelled. Almost as if everyone had decided to buy the same car and you started *noticing* them – all the time!

Now, you can exchange the car analogy for anything you like, for example, a woman planning for a baby starts noticing pregnant women while strolling down the High Street. It is also the same with advertising campaigns that subtly settle in your subconscious, and you start seeing the advertised product everywhere. The truth is these items are always going to be there – the car, the pregnant women, and the product – but your RAS cache is full of these searches, and your brain notices them when they are in your proximity. The RAS is a pattern searching machine that matches the reality outside your head with your 'cookies history' inside.

Remember the friend who proclaims, "Nothing good ever happens to me!" Well, guess what? Nothing good happens to them. But why is this so important? Consider for a moment your brain being a pattern-searching machine that you have pre-programmed deliberately to look for things to be grateful for. Everywhere you go your subconscious brain quietly searches for examples of all the things in your life that fill you with gratitude. Well, this is how, and more importantly why, a gratitude log works.

Reflection: Each day, list three things that you are grateful for (but you cannot repeatedly use the same items over and over). In doing so, your RAS will slowly start scanning for the examples of gratitude.

CHAPTER 73

The Performance Equation

"Only by great risks can great results be achieved."
– Xerxes I

Performance=Potential - Psychological Restrictions

Often, when I am working with clients, I aim to use simple, easy to implement, yet powerful tools. One of the tools that has served me well for many years is 'The Performance Equation', which is an iteration of a tool Timothy Gallway references in his best-selling book *The Inner Game of Tennis.*

In essence, you have your performance, which can be from any area of your life. It might be an event you have entered from a sporting perspective; it might be a presentation you were asked to give by your boss, or it might even be whether you were successful in a recent job interview. Although entirely different in context, all of these examples are measurable by the outcome metric that is your objective performance on the day. If you have no psychological restrictions on the day of the event, you will perform equal to your maximum potential by default. If you have any psychological restrictions, these will subtract from your potential and reduce the measurable performance.

All we can ever hope for is to perform equal to our potential in whatever we do.

So, what are some of these psychological restrictions I'm referring to? Well, it might not come as a surprise to you to find out there are a vast number of these restrictions, and we are all affected by them at different times, and in various areas of our life.

Poor Internal Dialogue

- Self-Limiting Beliefs
- Fear of Success
- Fear of Failure
- Mental Fatigue
- Poor Rehearsal
- Focus Loss / Concentration
- Poor Sleep
- Stress
- Pressure Perception
- Motivation Loss
- Confidence Loss

Each one of these elements can be improved through the endeavour of practice, commitment and application. Consider all the times you have been 'at your best' in any context – what were you thinking at the time? Consider likewise, the times when you have not performed to the standard you would have liked – which elements of this equation were in play that day? Perhaps you lost your focus right at the critical moment you needed to be laser-like? Maybe you were feeling stressed leading up to the event, and in turn, your sleep was severely reduced, leading to fatigue. What if it was a combination of poor internal dialogue that led to you creating the wrong mental pictures through visualisation. This may have led you to executing your negative visualisation flawlessly.

Reflection: These elements that sit within our psychological restrictions can be developed and strengthened with the correct application and practice over time. What must happen before practice is undertaken though, is an awareness of which parts affect you most frequently and in what context. With this elevated awareness, you can apply yourself to addressing the underlying factors that feed these psychological restrictions. Gradual, constant, incremental improvements over time will erode the restrictions allowing you to fully actualise your potential on the day of the performance.

CHAPTER 74

Stoic Principle – Time is More Precious Than Gold, Diamonds and Money

"Time is a storm in which we are all lost."
– William Carlos Williams

Time is such a mystical concept. In its most straightforward understanding, it is the ticking of a watch to prevent tardiness. At its most complicated, it is the relativity between the observer and the observed with the addition of gravity as a glue-like influence. It is something that surrounds us and permeates our daily lives, often without examination or evaluation. Time has the appearance of being linear – we move from the past to the present into the future as if we're walking a long, straight road – yet on closer examination, this linear perception is just a mirage. I cannot walk back to the past, and I cannot stroll ahead up the road of time with any certainty. In truth, the only thing that exists in relation to time is *now.*

We cannot touch, experience or influence anything from the past, so we can agree that the past no longer exists. Sure, you might remember the past, but you can't visit it like walking back down the straight road. The future lies ahead, but there is little certainty outside the basic presuppositions of events we all make, such as the sun disappearing as it drops beneath horizon only to re-emerge in accordance with the sunrise the following morning. We assume this to happen without much thought, but there is no certainty our predictions will come to pass.

So, if the future doesn't exist, likewise the past, why do we spend so much *time* living there in our head? Metaphorically speaking, of course.

Too often, we overly focus on future goals, like a three- or five-year plan. We can all be guilty of underappreciating the value of laying siege to today with purpose and decisiveness as if tomorrow doesn't exist. This is not to say setting goals is unimportant, but achieving goals relies on taking action, and this is always taken in the present moment.

By our nature, we are forward-looking, goal focused creatures that when glancing towards the next thing/moment/goal, often miss what is right in front of our eyes *now*. Learning to live in the present isn't complicated, but that doesn't mean it's easy. As a species, we either focus on the future, concentrating on what is yet to happen or ruminate about the past, wishing to change what cannot be changed. If repeated frequently enough, both patterns of thinking are roads to anxiety or depression depending on the direction of our focus.

Reflection: Instead of focussing on the years ahead, narrow your focus to a few months, then refocus again to the weeks, then zoom in on today, and finally on the minute you presently occupy. If you focus on winning these *moments*, by default you own time itself, as time is just a succession of moments consecutively arranged to give us a measurement of our subjective experience.

As an experiment, today constantly ask yourself these questions:

How can I appreciate this moment irrespective of its perceived irrelevance?

How can I get more from this moment?

Are the actions I'm taking right now moving me towards my goals?

The person who makes the best lemonade is the one who squeezes the most from their lemons.

CHAPTER 75

That Was a Bad Year!

"For us is the life of action, of strenuous performance of duty; let us live in the harness, striving mightily; let us rather run the risk of wearing out then rusting out."

– Theodore Roosevelt

Have you ever considered how odd it is of humans to attach so much meaning to objective measurement? For example, 2020 could genuinely be described as an 'annus horribilis', or a 'horrible year' in English. We endured the first wave of the Covid-19 pandemic, the Australian countryside burnt in a fire visible from space, protestors stormed the US Capitol Building under the 'loose' instructions of President Trump, all wrapped up in a global recession the likes of which made 2008 look affluent! 2020 was, without doubt, a year most would have looked forward to erasing from the memory and leaving in the past.

Another example of this obsession with measurements might be someone dreading passing a significant age milestone like forty, fifty, or perhaps sixty. It is as if this single rotation of the earth on its axis signifies the end of the life they had led till that point in time. It makes no sense if you stop for a moment to consider the absurdity.

If we were to apply this perspective in other areas, we would be met with some odd conclusions.

Consider for a moment, we have a bag of potatoes weighing 100kg, and inside the bag there is precisely 1kg of rotten potatoes. We might perhaps open the bag and remove the bad potatoes, but we would not necessarily attach the meaning of these bad potatoes to their weight representation. In truth, all the bad things that happened in 2020 were just events happening while our watery rock span through space, continually falling toward the sun but thankfully missing each time, continuing its elliptical gravity-fuelled orbital dance through the Cosmos.

In truth, we've been doing this since the cognitive revolution of our minds that some historians suggest started around 70,000 years ago during the last Ice Age. Consciousness gave us the ability to develop the concept of cause and effect from events that, in reality, were just happening in time and space, more often unconnected from other events.

Let's examine this further.

Consciousness gave rise to superstition, insomuch as humans started to believe supernatural influences were working in reality's shadows. Inanimate objects suddenly took on the personification of things they should either fear or worship, or perhaps both. Before humans developed a superstitious streak, if the moon was full and a cow died in the field during the night, they would not necessarily attach causation between the two. However, once superstition and abstract thinking arrived, if the cow died during the night and concurrently the moon was full, people might have reached for the conclusion that the cow died because the moon was full. From here there it is only a short leap to concluding that 'whenever the moon is full, cows will die'.

Reflection: Because we are meaning-seeking creatures, we often attach meaning to things that, in reality, have no actual meaning. Shaping your mindset to disconnect inherently unconnected events will help you towards the temperance we have discussed within many of these chapters.

CHAPTER 76

The Atomic Philosopher

"Nothing exists except atoms and empty space;
everything else is opinion."
– Democritus

The principal origins of Greek philosophy were to answer some fundamental existential questions: Where did we come from? Why are we here? What is reality, and what is it made of?

This last question is the one we shall focus on within this chapter as this is a question that defined most of the thinkers from antiquity. The original Greek philosopher is often acknowledged as Thales of Miletus. Aristotle regarded him as the Ionian school founder and suggested that Thales believed the original single substance was water. Pythagoras believed reality to be primordially made of numbers which he discerned from musical ratios. At first glance, this appears foolish until you consider how physicists represent their universal equations. Each ancient philosopher took it in turns to try and ascertain the original single substance, all that is except for Parmenides and his student Socrates. Parmenides believed reality to be illusory, so there seemed little reason to bother understanding the original singular substance of a grand hologram; I suspect this also influenced Socrates to focus on looking inside rather than outside.

The original atomic theorist was Democritus, who was a Greek philosopher living in the 5th century BC. Democritus derived his atomic theory from considering a stone that you might separate into two halves. If you were to keep repeating the process of halving the stone pieces, you would eventually arrive at an amount so small it would be indivisible or 'atomos', which is the Greek word for indivisible. Democritus believed that atoms were different in size and shape and were in constant motion, colliding with each other, and in colliding could either rebound or bind together. Because of these ideas, matter could by its very nature change and flux constantly.

A few centuries after Democritus, another Greek philosopher examined his ideas and dismissed them entirely; his name was Aristotle. Because of the considerable influence of Aristotle in his era, it was nearly 2,400 years before scientists revisited the concept of atoms comprising reality.

In 1905 Albert Einstein worked in a patent office in Berne, Switzerland. Although unknown before 1905, he announced his arrival onto the world stage of physics with a succession of brilliant papers challenging long-held beliefs. This year was so significant it is referred to in physics as 'Einstein's Annus Mirabilis', or 'his year of miracles' – there is a certain irony in this related to the previous chapter. The first paper would be his 'Special Theory of Relativity', which gave the world the most famous equation in science: $e=mc^2$. This later evolved into general relativity. Einstein's second groundbreaking paper in 1905 was a controversial proposal concerning the nature of light which latterly formed the basis for quantum theory. Finally, his third paper of 'annus mirabilis' paved the way for a crucial test of atoms' reality and thermodynamic laws' validity. Einstein theoretically proposed a mathematical calculation to determine the size of atoms in molecules. He achieved this by analysing sugar molecules dissolved in water; he calculated both the diameter of the molecule and Avogadro's number (the number of molecules per unit under standard condition). In doing this, Einstein proved Democritus correct about the nature of atoms. The interesting point here is the 2,400 years lost because of Aristotle's dismissal.

Reflection: Sometimes you have a belief so strong that no matter the resistance it burns as bright as ever. There have been numerous examples throughout history of a person's belief remaining steadfast, even against violence and ridicule. Democritus, Galileo Galilei, Nicolaus Copernicus, the Wright brothers, and Martin Luther King to name a few. They believed.

CHAPTER 77

I Can't Do That Here!

"The source from which existing things derive their existence is also that to which they return at their destruction."
– Anaximander

Gregory Bateson was an enigmatic lecturer at the University of California in Santa Cruz during the 1970s. Bateson was an anthropologist by training and taught a considerable scope of lectures to his students, ranging from communication theory to Maxwell's equations for electromagnetic fields, schizophrenia, and beyond. One of Bateson's theories was logical levels, influenced by Bertrand Russell's work in logic and mathematics. Bateson's work on logical levels was further developed by Robert Dilts, one of his students at the University of California.

Dilts developed a learning model he named 'Logical Levels of Therapy' which grouped certain 'classes' of thinking at different logical levels within the mind of a person, each level being *part* of, but not actually *being* that level. These levels do not only exist within our thinking but all around us in many contexts. Let me explain: if you are a student, you might be part of a class, and that class be part of a school, which might, in turn, be part of a larger campus, which in turn is part of an education system. Now, although the student is part of the class, the student is not the class. Likewise, the class is not the school etc. Bateson, and later Dilts, suggested that this occurs within our thinking at a neurological level. If we examine the statement below we can realise it has many meanings.

"I can't do this here."

1. ***(I)*** Identity
2. ***(Can't)*** Beliefs and Values
3. ***(Do)*** Capabilities
4. ***(This)*** Behaviour
5. ***(Here)*** Environment

Spiritual	**Vision and Purpose**	**For Whom? For What**
a. Who I am – Identity	Permission & Motivation	Who?
b. My belief system (Values)	Mission	Why?
c. My capabilities –	Maps & Plans	How?
d. What I do – Specific behaviours	Actions & Reactions	What?
e. My environment – External context	Constraints & Opportunities	Where? When?

Changes that are made at an upper level will cascade and affect levels below, precipitating change. Changing something at a lower level could, but not necessarily, affect the upper levels. These levels include (from highest to lowest):

There is also a sixth level which Dilts referred to as the 'Spiritual' level and is defined as a type of 'relational field' which gives a person a 'sense of belonging to a larger system beyond one's individual identity'.

Reflection: The purpose of understanding this model is to reflect on your challenges in life and identify which level of your thinking they are contained within. Knowing this is hugely valuable in allowing you to form a strategy and thus formulate solutions taking you beyond the boundaries of your problems; self-directing yourself towards what you want and away from what you do not.

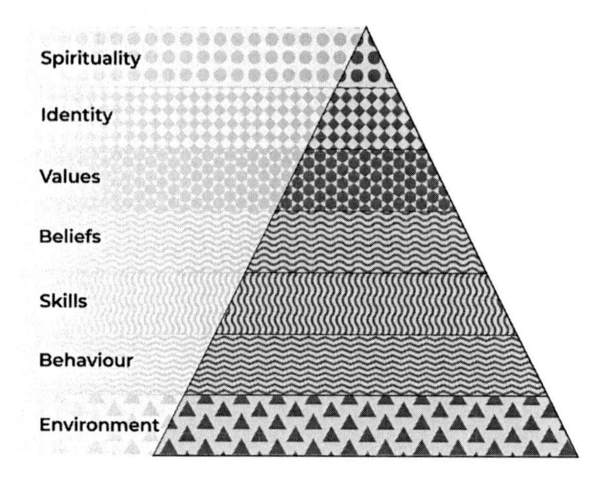

CHAPTER 78

The Two Monks

"I realise there's something incredibly honest about trees in winter, how they're experts at letting things go."
– Jeffrey McDaniel

Two wise monks walked silently together. One older and wiser monk, the teacher, and one younger monk, the apprentice. These holy monks belonged to a secular and deeply religious monastery and were observing the most sacred month of the year. During this month they had taken a vow of silence and a vow not to touch women.

As they walked together in silent contemplation, they approached a river which had risen quickly after the afternoon monsoon. A mother had become separated from her child on the other side of the river and was now panicking as the river was too strong for her to pass without help.

As the two monks approached, she begged for them to help.

The wise old monk contemplated and considered everything happening and the consequences of any action taken. He looked at the younger monk in silence, understanding the seriousness of breaking the holy vows. After a few moments of reflection, the wise old monk took the woman onto his shoulders, picked up a large branch for support and set about crossing the river. The young apprentice monk looked on with confusion, unsure what to make of his teacher breaking the holy vows of touch.

The river was difficult to cross, and the old monk battled with the strong flow of muddy water, which was nearly chest deep and at time perilously fast flowing. Following the old monk, the younger apprentice monk tried to understand the actions of his wise teacher. He appreciated the woman was in distress and understood the human element of what had occurred here, still, he simultaneously felt his teacher had desecrated their holy vows, which were more important than any act of compassion – regardless of the situation.

The crossing took nearly thirty minutes. Once they all finally reached the far riverbank, the wise teacher carefully placed the mother down on the firm ground. By this time, her child had arrived, and the newly reunited mother and child embraced in the way mothers and children do after being emotionally and physically separated.

The mother approached the wise monk, looked deep into his eyes and with tears of joy running down her cheeks, she gently kissed him and quietly said "thank you."

The wise monk smiled in return and gracefully bowed his head silently before carrying on his walk. All the while, the young apprentice observed in further disbelief.

The two monks carried on walking in silence for hours, but as time elapsed, the younger monk's internal struggle grew with each step. Finally, after hours of ruminating the young monk broke his silence and said; "Teacher, I do not understand. Today I have observed you breaking our holy vows and it troubles me greatly. I do not know what to think or feel?"

The wise monk looked silently at his young apprentice, contemplating his response.

"My brother, I did carry that woman across the river, you are correct, but I placed her down on the far side of the river. You have carried her since."

Credit: The Magic of the Metaphor. Nick Owen

Reflection: What are you still carrying unnecessarily that you could place down?

CHAPTER 79

Emotion = Chemicals

"The laws of nature are but the mathematical thoughts of the Gods."
– Euclid

In some previous chapters, I have mentioned my fiancée Ruth has a rare form of leukaemia that understandably plays a significant role in our lives. Because of this condition, she was understandably advised to shield during the Covid-19 pandemic; something which made complete sense. We were, however, unprepared for the rapid decline in her mental wellbeing over eight weeks in April and May 2020. Watching this unfold was very difficult and frustrating, and initially, I felt quite helpless. That was until we both decided to take action and start examining our daily habits and behaviours. From this experience, I decided to formalise what we had learned and created the 'Happy Chappy Guide' as a free resource to help others experiencing a circumstantial decline in their mental health caused by the challenges we were facing at the time. We were able to identify a handful of easy to implement, simple behaviours that positively impacted our wellbeing when implemented daily.

One of the topics we discussed was the role of chemicals, or hormones, in the brain and body and their relevance to general wellbeing and happiness. Hormones are chemicals produced by the various glands across your body. They travel through your bloodstream, acting as messengers and playing a vital role in many bodily processes. Specifically, we discussed four of these hormones that are often colloquially referred to as the 'happy hormones' as they contribute to positive mental health. What is even more interesting is the absence of these 'happy hormones' during isolation and lockdown scenarios such as the national lockdowns imposed during the Covid-19 pandemic.

Dopamine: Also known as the 'feel-good' hormone, dopamine is a hormone and neurotransmitter that is an essential part of your brain's reward system. Dopamine is associated with pleasurable sensations, along with learning, memory and motor system function. We are rewarded with dopamine when we partake in activities or experiences which we find enjoyable.

Oxytocin: Sometimes referred to as the 'love/cuddle hormone', it is essential for childbirth and all associated activities requiring human bonding, such as breastfeeding. This hormone also helps to promote trust and empathy in relationships. Oxytocin levels are elevated with physical contact and affectionate acts such as kissing, cuddling and sex.

Serotonin: This is a hormone and neurotransmitter, which helps regulate mood as well as your circadian rhythm (sleep patterns). It also plays a role in appetite, digestion, learning ability and memory. One of our primary sources of serotonin is Vitamin D, which is most naturally sourced from sunlight.

Endorphins: These are our natural pain relievers, which our body produces in response to any kind of physical exertion. Whenever we ask our bodies to work hard in any way, we increase our levels of endorphins, which have a legacy reward of 'feeling great' – as in the few hours after physical exercise.

Reflection: From looking at these hormones, what they are for, and how they are produced, you can immediately see the dangers of isolation and lockdown – the situation alone acts as a suffocating noose in the production of each one of these vital 'happy hormones'! Get outside in fresh air and sunlight, be active, connect with your loved ones and partake in the things that give you pleasure. All of these are choices you can make today.

CHAPTER 80

The Stomach in Your Brain

"Fate leads the willing and drags along the reluctant."
– ***Seneca***

Imagine for a moment, taking a mouthful of your favourite dish prepared by one of the finest chefs in the world. You might experience the flavours and textures arresting your senses as you savour the mouthful. The taste of each bite leaves behind a legacy of happiness as you look forward to the next mouthful and the sensory ecstasy it brings. Now, presuming they're different foods of course, imagine taking a mouthful of a greasy burger. You're aware it's not necessarily healthy and has little nutritional value, but you consume it anyway because it's a guilty pleasure and something you 'just can't resist'.

Finally, imagine eating a selection of healthily prepared vegetables; they do not give you the instant gratification of the burger or your favourite meal. They are often more challenging to consume, but you intuitively know that your body will be grateful for the nutrients and minerals provided by this meal.

Your subconscious mind consumes and digests information, in the same way your stomach consumes and digests nutrients. You may very well be aware of the news you watch consciously, absorbing the information via your visual and auditory senses. But what happens once this information passes by your conscious awareness? In truth, and in a similar non-experiential sense as your digestion, you are very much unaware of what happens past your senses, but that doesn't mean for a moment the process ends there. As your food is chewed then swallowed it continues its digestion process away from your awareness. So does the information that passes your conscious mind and carries on its 'cognitive digestion' at a deeper subconscious level, away from your conscious thought. But what does this mean for you?

The basis of all programming is to embed itself within your subconscious and influence your behaviour away from your conscious awareness. We mistakenly believe we are making our choices due to free will when our unconscious biases shape our every decision.

If Seneca were alive today, he might counsel against consuming too much information via news and social media, especially in the 'fake news' era we find ourselves in today.

We all understand that a diet of poor food will inevitably lead to poor health sooner or later – most likely sooner. This poor diet leading to poor health equation applies to our mental wellbeing and often with graver consequence from inaction. You can control the information flowing into and shaping your subconscious in the same way you might control and regulate your nutritional diet. With the application of discipline and commitment, you can control which information you expose your mind to and consume and digest. The ratio of good news versus bad news is not an accurate reflection of your reality. Still, your subconscious brain might start to accept the information as an accurate representation of your reality and start shaping your mind with beliefs in accordance with that information.

Reflection: From this day forward, I urge you to pay attention to the information you consume and understand that the digestion of this information goes past your sensory experience. By its very nature, it can shape and define the person you become tomorrow, for better or worse.

Poor nutritional diet > poor physical health.
Poor informational diet > poor mental health.

CHAPTER 81

Repetition, Repetition, Repetition (when you finish, start again)

"Give me six hours to chop down a tree and I will spend the first four sharpening the axe."
– Abraham Lincoln

As referred to in previous chapters we have developed a culture of immediacy in recent decades. Instant gratification has taken over from older ideals of perseverance and application, and the journey has been replaced by the teleportation to the final destination. This saddens me greatly. For thousands of years, sophists, philosophers and great thinkers have all known the reward of steadfast commitment towards mastery. I see the sacrifice of these ideals among many coaches who undertake their journey wanting to arrive at the destination before they've taken their first step. We want the 'noun', but not the 'verbs' which pave the way to the 'noun', which is similar to Chapter 52.

There is a straightforward formula for understanding progression (note the word progression, not perfection):

$$(\text{Experience} + \text{Reflection}) \times \text{Repetition} = \text{Progression}$$
$$(E + R) \times Rep = P$$

What is often missing from this formula from my observation is all three elements of this equation. Without all of these elements in place, which are the necessary ingredients for development, it is impossible to achieve meaningful progression.

An excellent quote is attributed to the great Roman Stoic philosopher, Seneca, *"Luck is what happens when preparation meets opportunity."*

Most of my adult life has been dedicated to understanding high performance in various guises. The pursuit of creating high performers has allowed me to observe and work with some of the highest performing humans, from multiple contexts. How do Olympic athletes cope with the pressure of an Olympic final? How do polar explorers have the resilience to withstand brutal conditions day after day to pursue their goals? What separates successful entrepreneurs from the many that are unsuccessful?

Multiple factors are at play with each of these questions, but there are also some common observable denominators.

These shared traits are where we can learn and then apply across any performance context.

These are the common traits I have observed:

Sacrifices: All the high performers I have coached have made constant sacrifices along the way. Whether that be missing social events or choosing to refrain from food, drink etc when they do attend. There is also the constant sacrifice of relentless travel which often appears exciting but in reality, is very repetitive and rarely offers the athlete any tourist type opportunities. They prioritise their work above nearly all other elements of life, often even intimate relationships. It is the things we're prepared to go without that are more important than the things we're prepared to do.

Repetition: Often, we mistakenly believe high performers practice complex skills every day. In my experience, this is not necessarily the case. More accurately, it's about doing the basics but repeatedly and better than anyone else – repetition, repetition, and repetition.

Self-Belief: This is a profound belief which surpasses confidence and is present throughout the journey. With self-belief, you can commit to the daily practice needed to achieve mastery. You can do this because deep down you have no doubt you can get to your goal, as long as you're prepared to keep going, keep moving forwards, no matter the situation or circumstance.

CHAPTER 82

The Seven Sages of Greece

"Seek to learn constantly while you live; do not wait in the faith that old age by itself will bring wisdom."
– *Solon*

Ancient Greece is renowned for producing some of the greatest thinkers the world has ever known. Perhaps there has been no other time in humanity's history where we have taken such intellectual leaps forward as the period between the 6th to the 1st century BC. Much of our modern culture was shaped by the ideas of these great minds. Whether it be Euclid with geometry, Pythagoras and his theorem, Hippocrates with medicine, Democritus and atoms, Socrates and dialect, or Plato and *The Republic*, Greek philosophers have shaped our entire existence. Sir Isaac Newton was also influenced by Greek Philosophy with his famous book *Philosophiæ Naturalis Principia Mathematica*, or the 'Mathematical Principles of Natural Philosophy'. Even amongst this grand history, there are 7 revered founding fathers, known as 'The Seven Sages of Greece'. It seems inconceivable that a book influenced so heavily by philosophy should not acknowledge some of antiquity's original thinkers.

Chilon of Sparta: Chilon was known as 'The laconic Spartan', and some historians attribute the most famous philosophical saying to him: "Know thyself." (This is contested, and many say Thales was the originator.) Chilon died from joy in the arms of his son, who had just won the Olympic games.

Bias of Priene: Bias was a preeminent lawyer and judge, and through an ironic twist, his name would, by coincidence, come to represent a person with 'unreasoned judgement and prejudice'. Bias wisely said he would rather decide a dispute between two of his enemies than two of his friends. He concluded this by logically stating that no matter what he ruled in the first case, one of his enemies would become his friend. Likewise for the second, no matter what he ruled one of his friends would become an enemy.

Pittacus of Mitylene: Pittacus was an odd sort of chap indeed. Often referred to as 'Sarapus' (because he was splay-footed), 'Gastron' (because he was fat) or 'Agasurtos' (because he was lazy and dirty). His most commonly attributed phrase is: "Know thine opportunity."

Solon of Athens: Solon was an Athenian statesman who laid the foundations for constitutional government, leading to classical Greek culture. Perhaps his most famous deed was repealing the laws of Dracon, which punished minor offences with death, and replacing it with a system in which only murder or manslaughter carried capital punishment. His most famous phrase was: "Nothing in excess."

Cleobulus of Lindos: Cleobulus was known to counsel, "When a man goes out of his house, he should consider what he is going to do when he returns home again, he should consider what he has done."

Thales of Miletus: Among these great minds, perhaps Thales is the best known and has the most extraordinary claim of greatness against his many achievements. He was the first recorded man in history to predict a solar eclipse (more about this in later chapters) and he is believed to have been the first man to have a specific mathematical equation attributed to him. If these achievements weren't enough, he also divided the calendar year into 365 days and determined the Great Pyramids of Egypt's heights by measuring the length of their shadows!

Periander of Corinth: Including Periander divides opinion as Plato left him off his original list of the Sages. He was as devious as he was clever. Perhaps the best example of this was his benevolent act of reducing the slaves in Corinth. This act was to ensure Corinthians would be too busy to conspire against him because of work.

Reflection: The very nature of human evolution allows the unusual ability to continually build upon the ideas and knowledge of those that came before, no other animal is afforded this intellectual *foot up.* From the geniuses that have already made their contributions awaits all the wisdom you could ever hope for, in the form of books. These books are all waiting for you to take the baton and run, waste no time in accepting the challenge.

CHAPTER 83

Trust

"Good actions give strength to ourselves,
and inspire good actions in others."
– Plato

A frog meets a scorpion on a riverbank. The scorpion is desperate to get to the other side and pleads with the frog to carry him across the river on his back. The frog is quite rightly suspicious of the scorpion and politely points out that it might sting him while swimming. The scorpion explains that he cannot swim and to sting the frog would result in death for them both. After some consideration, the frog decides to trust the scorpion and agrees to carry him to the other side. Halfway across the river, the scorpion inexplicably stings the frog, causing paralysis. As they both begin drowning the frog asks the scorpion why he's committed them both to death with his actions.

The scorpion replies, "I have no idea why, perhaps it's because I'm a scorpion?"

Credit: The Hunter of the Pamirs: A Novel of Adventure In Soviet Central Asia by Georgi Tushkan

Trust is a fascinating concept. Businesses are built upon it, relationships also. It can be lost in the blink of an eye and takes much more time to rebuild when betrayed. I have been too trusting in the past, without a doubt. It has only been in this year of my life when I have developed a cautiousness that prevents such mistakes. Everyone would act following their word in a utopian society, and trust would be an automatic starting point in any relationship. Unfortunately, in my experience, the reality is not reflective of this romantic ideal.

All is not lost, though. The key to building more robust and resilient relationships is to invest heavily in building trust. Whether in business or your personal relationships, investment in this area will lead to astounding results over time. One of the finest models for understanding the underpinning value of trust is Patrick Lencioni's '5 Dysfunctions of a Team'. Don't be discouraged by the title; books often use negative titles as they market better than positive titles. What Lencioni talks about in his book is the 5 fundamental functions of a high performing team. The model is built like a pyramid with each level underpinning and supporting the level above. Unsurprisingly, the underpinning foundations of the entire model's first level is trust.

The absence of trust will catastrophically undermine all the other levels above. Often when I'm working with organisations, nearly all of their challenges have their origins in trust, or lack of it to be more accurate. Unfortunately, there are no shortcuts or hacks for building trust with individuals, especially if those individuals don't necessarily like each other, which is often the case within organisations. The starting point for me is to have the courage to show vulnerability, which is often feared most when trust is missing, both professionally and personally. It is easy to understand when trust is present, because honest debate and conflict can occur without being perceived as an agenda-based interaction with ulterior meanings.

Reflection: If you can do this, you're well on the way to establishing a high performing team. If conflict and debate cannot be honest and without agenda, you have to step back down to the trust level and start again with vulnerability.

RESULTS

ACCOUNTABILITY

COMMITMENT

CONFLICT

TRUST

CHAPTER 84

The Frog & The Fish

"What worries you, masters you."
–John Loke

There was once a pond which was the shape of a box and had been dug by the hand of man many years before and left abandoned. Over time nature had taken over where man had left off, and the box pond was now full of life and covered with wonderful lily pads offering cover and protection to the fish who swam below. In the pond, there was a baby tadpole and a baby fish born around the same time. The baby tadpole and fish immediately became great friends and would go everywhere in the pond together; they were inseparable like best friends often are. Slowly they both started to change, growing and evolving. The fish, although changing and increasing in size, remained a fish. The young tadpole, however, was transforming into a young frog. The frog and fish remained best friends nonetheless and still loved exploring the box pond.

One day, the frog had an idea and proposed to the fish, "I know. Let's go and explore outside the pond!"

The fish looked back at the frog in disbelief. "But we cannot go outside the safety of the pond; unimaginable dangers are waiting outside the pond. I have heard stories. It's just not safe."

"I know there are stories," replied the frog. "But we must go because there are also stories of adventures beyond our wildest imaginations. We have explored inside the pond so much now there is nothing left to discover. Because of this alone we have to set our sights on new adventures and new discoveries."

But no matter what the frog said to the fish, he could not convince his friend to embark on this new adventure together. After days of trying to persuade the fish to join him, he resigned himself to his fate. He had to go solo for this adventure if he was to go at all. With a heavy heart, the frog said goodbye to his friend and leapt from the box pond. Without his friend to explore the pond, the fish was lost, and although he would still explore the corners of the pond, it seemed less adventurous without his friend.

Days went by, and the fish went from missing his friend to worrying if he might ever return. One day, with a tumultuous splash, the frog re-entered the pond. Excitedly, the fish commanded the frog to tell him everything about his solo adventure. The frog, anxious to share all of the details, responded with, "Well, outside the pond there are these amazing things called flowers with bright colours!"

The fish responded; "What the hell are flowers?"

The frog, undeterred, quickly responded; "Never mind the flowers, there are also huge trees reaching high towards the sky and clouds!"

Once more confused, the fish replied, "What the hell are trees, and while we're on it, what is sky and clouds?"

The frog, unsure what to say next considered his following words, "Well, fish, I suppose in many ways the world outside the pond is the same as in here, except outside the pond there is no water."

Still, with a confused expression which seemed to deepen further, the fish replied; "What the hell is water, Frog?"

Credit: The Magic of the Metaphor, Nick Owen

Reflection: Like with many chapters we explore the concept of how our beliefs at some level create our reality, this Is true in the simplest example of the things we either choose to do, or not. This story reminds me fondly of my wonderful friend, Andrew Morris. Andy was certainly the frog who quite literally jumped at any opportunity, he once tried to convince me to ride a bike around the world with him, it was a leap too large for me personally.

CHAPTER 85

Stoic Principle – Read with Purpose and Apply Your Knowledge

"Don't just say you have read books. Show that through them you have learned to think better, to be a more discriminating and reflective person. Books are the training weights of the mind. They are very helpful, but it would be a bad mistake to suppose that one has made progress simply by having internalised their contents."

– ***Epictetus, The Art of Living***

We have discussed in previous chapters the modern pursuit of destination before the journey. This concept also applies to reading. I mistakenly believed I was unintelligent, and from the moment I left high school till the age of thirty – some fourteen years – I did not read. It only took a single book to ignite my curiosity, and once lit, it has only grown stronger over the years. There seems to be an explosion of courses you can attend, which teach you to speed read books at a rate of an entire book per week, and sometimes faster. I believe this to be another wonderful example of modern humans attaching the cart before the horse.

Epictetus explains in his wonderful quote above that it is not just about saying you have read 50 books per year if you haven't retained or understood and practically applied the knowledge. This is just peacock feathering of the highest order.

Would it not be better to read ten books per year which you fully absorb and understand, than just to claim you have read fifty when more accurately you have held fifty books in your hands over this period?

This echoes back to this ridiculous element of modernity where people tend to leapfrog their journey to arrive at the destination. They're so focused on the outcome they miss the purity of the experience itself.

Books are the training weights of the mind.

When you fully absorb yourself into a book metaphorically, by default you reciprocate the neurological absorption of the text into the synapses of your mind. New connections are forged while exploring concepts and ideas that, in turn, create brand new neural pathways in the brain. You're taking your mind to the gym as Epictetus wonderfully describes above.

In my experience, the pathway to mastery is by becoming the best student. I am currently walking this path myself in my pursuit of understanding the many elements of breathwork. My reading list is now primarily focused on that specific area with books by Dan Brule, Stig Severinsen, James Nester, Stanislav Grof and Wim Hoff. It is not about reading these books as fast as I humanly can so I can claim to my friends I have read them, it is about deep diving into the subject and expanding my thinking as much as possible.

Reflection: Consider the last book you read and reflect on how deeply you understood the text. (Obviously not so relevant for novels and fiction. After this, when you undertake your next book, do not finish the book as fast as possible, instead focus on the pursuit of deep understanding of the ideas and concepts and how you can apply the knowledge to your life.

"A house that has a library in it has a soul."
– Plato

CHAPTER 86

The Roman Three – Seneca & Epictetus

"It is impossible for anyone to learn that which he thinks he already knows."
*– **Epictetus***

Stoicism originated with Zeno teaching his version of philosophy from the Stoa Poikile (painted porch) in 304 BC. Much of the early writings of Stoicism were lost through the centuries with the passage of time. Hundreds of years later Stoicism experienced a revival, thanks mainly to three Romans: Seneca the Younger, Epictetus and Marcus Aurelius.

Lucius Annaeus Seneca the Younger was the first in the trilogy. He was a philosopher, lawyer, statesman, dramatist, and political advisor. Although considered Roman, Seneca the Younger was born in Corduba, Spain. He was the son of Seneca the Elder, who was a wealthy and learned writer in his own right. Seneca the Elder tasked Attalus to educate the young Seneca, and the youthful philosopher in waiting took to the classroom with vigour. Attalus believed that the purpose of study was to ensure that each day you "return home a sounder man, or at least on the way to becoming a sounder man".

Seneca the Younger lived through turbulent times in Rome and spent many years exiled by either his health or the whims of various Emperors over time. Suffering from a severe lung condition in his early 20s, Seneca retreated to Egypt to recover, which took nearly ten years. In this time, he read ferociously as he moved further from being the lawyer Seneca the Elder had hoped, toward the philosopher his father did not want.

In 41 AD the new emperor, Claudius, exiled Seneca, who was now living back in Rome. During this exile, Seneca started a life-long love of letter writing, and nearly 2,000 years later, *Letters From Seneca* are seminal pieces of Stoic philosophy. After eight years of exile on Corsica at the behest of Claudius, Agrippina, the mother of the future emperor, Nero, recalled Seneca back to Rome. Seneca's role was to tutor the young emperor in waiting. Unfortunately, Nero became one of the most tyrannical Emperors and joined Caligula (37–41 AD), Commodus (180–192 AD), Caracalla (198–217 AD), and Maximus Thrax (235–238 AD) as the famous five worst Emperors of Rome. Seneca was eventually forced to commit suicide by Nero in 65 AD. Seneca was likely innocent of Nero's accusations that he conspired with others to assassinate the emperor.

Epictetus was born in 50 AD and would have been around fifteen years old when Seneca took his own life. There is little chance Epictetus would have been aware of Seneca's ill fate at this early age. Epictetus was born into slavery in Phrygia, which is modern-day Turkey. Ironically, it was Nero's decree that no slave be released until past his 30th birthday which eventually offered freedom for Epictetus. Epictetus' master was Epaphroditus, who was a slave himself initially, before being granted freedom by Nero for revealing a possible coup against the emperor.

On release from slavery, Epictetus studied with the great Stoic teacher, Musonius Rufus, who immediately recognised the potential of the former slave. Eventually, Epictetus set up his school of Stoic Philosophy and taught there until he, alongside the other Roman philosophers, was banished by the emperor, Domitian, in the year 89 AD. After exclusion from Rome, Epictetus travelled to Nicopolis in Greece to teach Stoicism until he died in 130 AD.

Discourses and Selected Writings, Epictitus

Enchridion, Epictitus

CHAPTER 87

The Roman Three – Marcus Aurelius

"That things have no hold on the soul. They stand there unmoving, outside it. Disturbance comes only from within – from our own perception."
– *Marcus Aurelius, Meditations 4.3*

It seems appropriate to dedicate an entire chapter to the great Roman Emperor, Marcus Aurelius, predominantly as his philosophy has guided and shaped many other pages within this book. Whether by gentle influence or using many of his quotations from his book *Meditations*, Marcus Aurelius is a true great of Stoicism, leadership and mindset.

Marcus Aurelius is often referred to as the last of the 5 'good' Emperors of Rome, representing the Roman Empire's golden era. These 5 good emperors were Nerva (reigned 96–98 AD), Trajan (98–117 AD), Hadrian (117–138 AD), Antonius Pius (138–161 AD), and finally Marcus Aurelius (161–180 AD).

Source: Chronicle of the Roman Emperors, Thomas Hudson

Marcus Aurelius is perhaps best known for his keen interest in philosophy, in particular Stoicism. His character is more widely known from the Ridley Scott film, *Gladiator*, where he is depicted accurately in the early parts of the film before dying on the Northern front and passing rule to his son Commodus. It probably comes as no surprise that the Hollywood depiction has historical inconsistencies, specifically Commodus' murdering his frail father. By this point, Marcus was already dying from the plague and Commodus had been named Caesar (heir to the throne) for several years already. Because of this it is improbable he would have murdered his father and risked his reign in doing so. Another important element left out of the movie was Marcus' brother, Lucius Verus, who co-ruled successfully alongside him. Lucius died in 169 AD. Both Marcus and his brother were adopted.

Throughout his life, Marcus Aurelius had to deal with tragedy and adversity. Whether through the loss of many of his children (believed to be between seven and nine), or his often frail and failing health, Marcus Aurelius embodied unwavering Stoic principles.

Perhaps the most fitting way to encapsulate Marcus Aurelius' character is to allow him to speak with his own words:

"The time of a man's life is as a point; the substance of it ever flowing, the sense obscure; and the whole composition of the body tending to corruption. His soul is restless, fortune uncertain, and fame doubtful; to be brief, as a stream so are all the things belonging to the body; as a dream, or as a smoke, so are all that belong unto the soul. Our life is a warfare, and mere pilgrimage. Fame after life is no better than oblivion. What is it that will adhere and follow? Only one thing; philosophy. And philosophy doth consist in this, for a man to preserve that spirit which is within him, from all manner of contumelies and injuries, and above all pains or pleasures; never do anything either rashly, or feignedly, or hypocritically: only to depend from himself, and his own proper actions: all things happen unto him to embrace contentedly, as coming from him from whom he himself also came; and above all things, with all meekness and a calm cheerfulness, to expect death, as being nothing else but the resolution of those elements themselves suffer nothing by their perpetual conversion of one into another, that dissolution, and alteration, which is so common unto all, why should it be feared by any? Is not this in according to nature? But nothing that is according to nature can be evil."

Reflection: Epistemology is the study of the origins of knowledge and to truly understand the development of Stoicism, as well as other schools of Greek philosophy, you have to travel back in time to its earliest origins. Reading the work of all three of the Roman Stoics will indeed prove a wise use of time.

CHAPTER 88

Pneuma (Part 1 – The Stoics)

"Philotimo to the Greek is like breathing.
A Greek is not a Greek without it."
*– **Thales***

The average respiratory rate of a modern human is approximately sixteen breaths per minute, which equates to 960 breaths per hour and around 23,000 breaths every single day, depending on our subjective activity, of course. Many of us take for granted the very breath that sustains our life force. I also did, until just over four years ago when I understood the vitality and importance of breathing. We do not breathe efficiently at all.

I now consider myself a student of breath, and because the topic is so vast and deep, I have allocated four chapters to this topic in succession. In truth, this will barely scratch the surface, and I urge you to pursue the study of breath through dedicated books to the subject (my recommended list at the end of this section). Pneuma (Greek) is inextricably intertwined with religion and spiritualism from various cultures. In Hebrew tradition, where Greek was used, Pneuma stood for life, spirit, consciousness, and angels and demons of invisible nature. In John 4:24 of the *New Testament*, it is unusually used to describe God himself: "God is spirit, and his worshippers must worship in the Spirit and in truth."

Pneuma, or 'spirit', originates from the Greek verb 'pneo', which indicates breathing or blowing. Since breathing is a necessity of life, the word became multi-functional to describe thoughts and sensations and non-human uses like the wind. Pneuma also adopted a cosmological dimension as some philosophers believed it held vital importance, especially the Stoic philosophers. Stoics thought that Pneuma was the beginning and the end of the Cosmos, the alpha and omega, the light and the dark.

The fundamental cosmology which underlies Stoic philosophy is built upon three core principles (Taylor & Francis, 1998):

- **Materialism:** The agreement that everything in the Cosmos is made of matter. This matter is made of a primordial substance which the Stoics believed was Pneuma. This illuminates the importance of Pneuma to the Stoics insomuch as everything in the known universe contains this primitive element.

- **Dynamism:** Because the Cosmos contains material bodies, all that exists has the ability of both acting and being acted upon. This cosmologically separates existence into two parts; a passive part which is substance, and an active part which gives it quality. For example, a flower only becomes a flower because it contains the bodily attributes within itself. The universal reason, Logos, guides nothing in this system, and everything.
- **Monism:** Any position related to singularity, or oneness, may be referred to as Monism. If Materialism (Pneuma) is the thesis, and Dynamism (Logos) the antithesis, then Monism is the synthesis which connects, binds and bonds the previous two principles together.

So fundamentally, according to the Stoics, Pneuma is the primordial substance of the Cosmos which builds all matter, a single principle. Logos then guide this matter. Both Pneuma and Logos come together in synthesis by divine Nature, or God – Monism.

We might espouse that these esoteric ideas bear little resemblance to our modern astrological understanding about the working of the universe, or we might just embrace them metaphorically rather than literally. When we do this, they take on a wonderfully imaginative meaning and allow us to glimpse into the minds of the ancient Stoics.

CHAPTER 89

Pneuma (Part 2 – My Introduction to Wim Hof)

"Breathe motherfucker!"
– Wim Hof

In earlier chapters, I briefly mention embarking on my journey to explore the Wim Hof Method (WHM). Also, in those previous chapters, I encouraged you to commit to taking some cold showers and researching the Wim Hof method more acutely outside the pages of this book. Once again, I hope you accepted this invitation. In a world where prescription medicine addiction is rising at a breath-taking pace, specifically in the areas of chronic pain management, anxiety disorders, depression and sleeping disorders, why would we not embrace approaches that are non-medicated, wholly natural and require very little training? I should be clear from the outset to avoid any ambiguity: I am in no way insinuating that breathwork and cold-water therapy solves and cures all ills – that would be both erroneous and irresponsible. I am claiming it can help in many areas, and without doubt, the WHM contains peer-reviewed science, gathering momentum as time evolves.

The best way for me to write about this method is through the lens of personal experience, rather than diving deep into science. At the end of this book, I have included a comprehensive list of scientific research resources should you like to broaden and deepen your understanding.

As mentioned in Chapter 23, my journey with the WHM began with a case of mild burnout, which occurred in October 2017. I had finished a gruelling period of teaching at our Academy. The relentless teaching schedule, without a break, was accompanied by a customary couple of beers or bottle of wine in order to unwind at the end of a long day's training. The alcohol prevented the deep sleep I desperately needed for my mind and coupled with an over-indulgence of coffee to maintain my energy levels, I was unwittingly creating the perfect storm for burnout to occur – and occur it most certainly did. On the last day of the final course, I felt understandably exhausted, both physically and mentally. Driving home, it was challenging to keep my eyes open, and the only thing I could think about was finally getting home and sleeping. What I didn't know at this point was I would be unable to function correctly for nearly two weeks! During this period of forced inactivity, I stumbled across this rather eccentric Dutch guy called Wim Hof, or the 'Ice Man'. What began with watching YouTube videos progressed to reading books, which further led to researching the scientific evidence supporting Wim's claims. I was astounded there was so much credible science to support the claims that Wim made.

The claims that Wim made that fascinated me the most were around influencing the autonomic nervous system, not only for himself but also for twelve students who had completed ten days of training with Wim in preparation. For the experiment, there was a control group (n=12) and a trained group (n=12). The ten-day training for the trained group consisted of meditation (third eye meditation), breathing techniques (cyclic hyperventilation followed by breath retention), and immersion in cold water. Both subjects underwent experimental endotoxemia (i.v. administration of *Escherichia coli* endotoxin). The trained group was able, via the breathing techniques, to generate significantly increased epinephrine levels, which resulted in significantly lower levels of flu-like symptoms.

(Voluntary activation of the sympathetic nervous system and attenuation of the Innate Immune response In humans, Matthijis Kox, Lucas T. van Eijk, Peter Pickkers)

Reading this was just the start of the journey for me; I needed to experience the benefits myself.

CHAPTER 90

Pneuma (Part 3 – Meeting the Cold)

"The cold is an absolute doorway to the soul."
*– **Wim Hof***

Once I had read the books and watched the videos, I needed to put into action the WHM and experience it myself. One of the most beautiful things about Wim's approach is its relative simplicity. You can search on YouTube and find numerous videos that allows you to experience three rounds of the breathing technique as an example.

The Wim Hof Method is separated into three pillars which can be undertaken individually but when brought synergistically together are an incredibly formidable combination:

1. **Breathwork:** The WHM is a combination of cyclic hyperventilation, often around thirty breaths, followed by breath retention, undertaken after the final out breath. Each person determines the period of re-

tention, and the idea isn't to push yourself to extremes, to the point where you desire a breath and do so. This would constitute one round of the breathing, and often it is repeated for anything between three to ten rounds depending on the breather's experience. Many people find they can hold their breath for much longer than they had initially believed before starting the method. I was dumbfounded at the speed of improvement with my breath hold over a very short length of time. Within only a few months, my breath hold had increased to four minutes and fifty seconds without placing undue duress on myself in the process.

2. **Cold Water:** The element of the WHM which most intimidates beginners is the notion of intentionally going into cold water. For some of us, our upbringing has left us with many misconceptions about the effect of cold water. Because of this parental conditioning, we often erroneously believe that cold water will make us ill. It should be emphasised from the outset that cold water injuries, such as hyperthermia, are very much given the respect they deserve. The approach with the WHM is "gradual, non-forced cold exposure". The science behind the method suggests only two minutes is required to receive all the benefits of the practice. After two minutes 'the law of diminishing returns' takes hold, which states that

there will be no further increase in the returning benefit after a designated point, which is two minutes with the WHM. My personal experience is that the body and mind quickly condition themselves to the cold environment. In a surprisingly short period, what starts as extremely uncomfortable, quickly becomes very comfortable.

3. **Commitment:** This entire book is built upon the necessity of applying commitment if you hope for any positive returns. It is not, and never will be, enough to intellectually theorise about the ideas and concepts without putting them into action experientially. Imagine learning to swim without ever getting into the water. Wim believes that we have become addicted to our comfort, and this same addiction is creating many of the modern challenges of the body and mind we face today. This is a theory I subscribe to entirely. Developing a mindset of commitment and growth can be developed over time, and it is certainly not the case that you are either born with a mind like Wim or you are not. It starts with a simple decision: "I will practice the breathing and turn my shower from hot to cold." Once you have done this on day one, repeat the next day.

I discovered many benefits from practising this breathing method. Scientists such as Professor Andre Huberman from the Huberman Lab are now to helping develop the research to support the anecdotal claims that the WHM helps to reduce inflammation, improve mood, and a boost immune system, as well as reconnecting humans with nature. Try it – today!

CHAPTER 91

Pneuma (Part 4 – The Origins & Development of Breath)

"Act, speak, and think like a man ready to depart this life in the next breath."
– Marcus Aurelius

Once I experienced the benefits of exploring breathwork from using the WHM, my mind started to wonder what other breathwork types were available, and what might their benefits be. I was to quickly find out that I was just starting my journey into the breath. Many visionaries and pioneers have been developing different breathwork approaches worldwide, some of them for decades now, notably Stig Severinsen, Wim Hof, Dr Stanislav Grof, Dan Brulee and Gitan Tonkov (to note only a few). In truth, many of these amazing people are building upon ancient knowledge that has been handed down, sometimes over thousands of years.

So where do we start this journey?

Pranayama: It is challenging to pinpoint the origins of many modern approaches to working with the breath with any degree of accuracy. One of the oldest known sources is Pranayama which is at least 5,000 years old but may be as old as 10,000 years old depending on which historical text you study. Modern Pranayama is based within Yoga Sutras today and was first recorded around 200–300 BC by Patanjali.

'Prana', which means energy in Sanskrit and 'Yama' which means control or restraint, illustrates the approach. The various techniques within Pranayama control the airflow in and out of the body. Some of the methods, such as Omkar, Ujjayi and Kumbhaka reduce airflow rate, which results in CO_2 levels rising and O_2 levels dropping. In Kumbhaka, there is no airflow, resulting in a more dramatic increase in CO_2 and a reciprocal decrease in O_2. Other techniques, such as Kapalbhati and Bhastrika focus on the opposite rise in O_2 and decrease in CO_2.

Breathology: Breathology was developed by 4x Freediving World Champion and multiple World Record Holder, Stig Severinsen. The Breathology methodology is built upon three specific principles:

1. The art and science of breath control and yoga.
2. Research on human physiology and neurology.
3. Modern sport exercise training and FLOW psychology.

Like many modern approaches to breathwork, Stig draws on older knowledge from a variety of sources. Specifically, Breath Holding (Apnea Training), Coherent Breathing (Valsalva Wave), Hypercapnic Training (Buteyko), Pranayama Breathing (Yogic Tradition), Holotropic Breathwork (Transformational Breathwork) and Hyperventilation Breathing (Tummo Meditation).

There are many other approaches to breathwork, and in my experience, they are all as fascinating as each other. I constantly refrain from making wild statements about anything, instead preferring to allow the experiences to speak for themselves. However, I am comfortable stating that the power of breathwork cannot be emphasised enough. To start your breathwork journey today it takes only the commitment to doing some research. Many approaches, such as the Wim Hof method, can begin by simply downloading an app or watching Wim on YouTube. Above anything else I have tried in my life, breathwork has been the most significant single gamechanger. I don't think I can say any more except for echoing Wim's wise words: *"Breathe motherfucker!"*

CHAPTER 92

The Spartan Agoge

"The mind is not a vessel to be filled but a fire to be kindled."
– Plutarch

Becoming a Spartan warrior was not an automatic right of young Spartan boys. It was a long and brutal regime of training conducted over their entire development, spanning approximately thirteen years from start to finish.

Staring at the age of seven, young Spartan boys wore only a simple cloak with no shoes to denote their novice status. They would also have their heads shaved and only be allowed to bear a sickle as a weapon. Rites of passage were not guaranteed, and tests and trials were frequent to ensure the correct standards were met. Included within the young Spartan boys' education was physical education, reading, writing, dancing, philosophy, logic and rhetoric.

As the Spartan boys approached adolescence, they transitioned to a new phase of their Agoge. Hair was permitted to grow to represent their growing status, and the physical training also grew with intensity. Within this peer group, the young boys were separated into different age classes, each with older Spartan boys to oversee their younger peer groups, ensuring standards were maintained. This developmental training wasn't just restricted to physical and martial skills; Spartan manners were also held in high regard. The young adolescents would be introduced to the ways of young Spartan gentlemen. This would include keeping their hands inside their robes while in public, walking without talking, and keeping their eyes always on the ground. All of this was under the scrutiny of established Spartan warriors who would take sport in testing the young Spartan boys on their knowledge and capabilities.

As the boys approached the age of manhood, from between eighteen to twenty, the training would once again increase with intensity. Mock battles were introduced for the first time alongside the weapons of the Spartan soldier.

The final phase of the Agoge was known as the Krypteia, the name deriving from 'secret' or 'hidden'. For one entire year, the twenty-year-old Spartan would have to live completely secluded from the Polis. He had to survive entirely off the land and never be seen by any of Sparta's general population. He was outcast like a ghost. With no shoes, bedding, or food, the aspirant Spartan soldier had to be completely self-sufficient, relying on stealth, resourcefulness, resilience, and fortitude. Should he emerge triumphant from this year-long trial, he could then call himself a true Spartan warrior.

Reflection: We are all on our Agoge; it is all the trials of your life so far. When you look deeply into the Spartan culture, there is much to be desired when measured against our modern societies' laws and customs. This does not preclude us the opportunity of taking the best elements and moulding their philosophy into our current way of living. There was a good reason the Spartan Agoge was so long, arduous, and brutal. The Spartans wanted fierce warriors who had endurance and resilience; they knew the only way to create their iconic soldiers was with suitably iconic preparation.

I believe we can all benefit from improving our resilience; there have been numerous chapters in this book where we have explored this concept. It is now down to you to take these ideas and commit yourself to taking action towards starting your personal Agoge.

CHAPTER 93

Thales and the Battle That Never Was

"What is it that is most beautiful? The Universe; for it is the work of God. What is most powerful? Necessity; because it triumphs over all things. What is most difficult? To know one's self. What is most easy? To give advice."

– Thales of Miletus

In the year 585 BC the ancient Lydians (ancient Turks) and the Medes (ancient Iranians) had been at war for six years. At this point, there was no clear victor in sight as each country exchanged dominance back and forth. A famous Meletian philosopher named Thales of Miletus, had recently made a bold prediction. Within the year the day would be turned to night and signify the end of the war. On the afternoon of May 28th, 585 BC, this came to pass, and both sides laid down their weapons and called a truce.

This was the first recorded solar eclipse prediction of the ancient world. It wasn't until 150 BC (some 400 years later) before the next recorded eclipse prediction by Hipparchus (the philosopher who also discovered trigonometry). But was this 585 BC prediction an act of genius, a wonderous mistake, or perhaps blind luck? In truth, it divides historians on which of these three options occurred, and realistically we shall not know for certain. I choose to believe in his brilliance; after all, Thales did accurately measure the heights of the pyramids and was one of the Seven Sages of Greece in antiquity.

We first heard of this incredible solar eclipse prediction by the Greek historian, Herodotus. Herodotus lived around 100 years after Thales, so a considerable amount of time had elapsed from the event, which sometimes casts doubt on accuracy. Added to this in 585 BC, Mesopotamian astronomers had not yet figured out how to use Saros cycles to make such predictions with any accuracy. Supposing Thales was to have made this claim, it almost certainly would have been learned under the tutorage of ancient Babylonians who were based near modern-day Baghdad. The Babylonians were known to keep incredibly accurate records of the planetary movements in the sky. As early as 1063 BC they had documented recording on ancient tablets of a total eclipse "that turned day into night". The discovery of Saros cycles, which governs the recurrence of eclipses and enables predictions, was born from these observations. Imagine for a moment the wonder as the entire field of battle fell under the path of totality, turning what was a sunny day into nightly shadow.

In antiquity, solar and lunar eclipses would have represented mystical, spiritual and religious significance. The prediction of this event for the first time would have been viewed in complete wonderment. Without doubt, it is a testament to this wonderment that precipitated the laying down of arms between armies which had fought incessantly for nearly six years.

Another element to this fascinating story is the element that led to the scepticism amongst some historians. Herodotus writes: "Thales of Miletus had foretold this loss of daylight to the Ionians, fixing it within the year in which the change did indeed happen." Astronomy is a precise science. If the knowledge existed to make such a prediction, it would undoubtedly have been more accurate than to offer a year window for the prediction to come to pass. This, suggest some historians, points to either a possible fluke or that the story evolved into a myth from an event that did not occur.

Reflection: As stated though, I prefer to believe that Herodotus was indeed correct in his writing and war was halted because of the mind of a single man, albeit an incredibly intelligent one at that.

CHAPTER 94

The Tinsmith And The Prison

"To know that you are a prisoner of the mind is the dawn of wisdom."
– Sri Nisargadatta Maharaj

A long time ago in the deserts of North Africa, there lived a simple tinsmith. The tinsmith was skilled and gifted with his hands; it was said he could make anything requested from metal. He and his wife lived a simple life, both profoundly religious God-fearing people. One day the tinsmith was accused of a crime of thievery by a local trader, something emphatically denied by the honest tinsmith. Although the evidence was circumstantial and hearsay, the tinsmith was unable to afford representation because of his modest savings. He found himself in the terrible position of being an innocent man unable to adequately prove his innocence to the courts.

Once the arguments had been heard the day of judgement arrived. The tinsmith, although innocent, was found guilty of all charges. During these times, sentences were often harsh, and thievery was offered little mercy once the accused was convicted. The tinsmith was sentenced to many years imprisonment and was only spared a much harsher sentence in light of his exemplary character and devotion to his religion.

As well as being a deeply religious man, the tinsmith was also sharp of mind to match his skill with his hands. He was not about to let his situation better him and immediately set about the task of making the most of his incarceration. He closely examined all of the choices within his influence and set about making his life more comfortable within the prison. The jail was secure, and the guards vigilant to their duty, but this did not deter the tinsmith from dreaming of escape for he had no desire to remain in prison for the rest of his life.

One day his wife brought him a prayer mat, and every day, five times per day, he prayed on it.

After some time had passed the tinsmith suggested to the guards, "I am poor and most likely will spend my remaining years within these walls. You too are poor and work long hours for a modest return; perhaps we can help each other?"

The tinsmith continued, "I am a tinsmith by trade, and although my skill remains sharp, I have no basic materials nor simple tools to complete my work. If you saw fit to provide me with both, I can make goods that you could sell for profit at the local market. My reward is to put to use my God-given talent, and your reward will be the profit from the market sales."

The guards cautiously agreed with the tinsmith's proposal. Soon the tinsmith was producing beautiful artefacts, and the guards were supplementing their meagre wages with healthy profits from selling the antiques at the market. This symbiotic relationship carried on for the next six months, uninterrupted.

One day, the guards awoke the inmates as they did each morning. Only on this morning, the cell that contained the tinsmith was empty. The door was locked, the bars intact, and there were no signs of escape from tunnels nor holes. It was as if the tinsmith had vanished without a trace. Soon, the tinsmith legend started to evolve with many suggesting he was, in fact, a magician not a tinsmith.

After many years there had been no sign, nor word, of the tinsmith or indeed of his family who had vanished at the same time. The king had often wondered about how the tinsmith disappeared but could not explain. Coincidently, a well-known criminal was found guilty of many crimes. On hearing his sentence of life imprisonment, the criminal turned to religion and admitted guilt to a great many unsolved crimes, including the crime committed by the tinsmith. As soon as the king heard of the admission of guilt from the criminal, he immediately pardoned the tinsmith and sent word to the farthest parts of his kingdom that the tinsmith and his family were free to return to their hometown and hitherto granted a full royal pardon.

Word quickly reached the tinsmith, and upon hearing, he immediately set about the long journey to his home province. Once he and his family arrived back to a hero's welcome from their friends and family, the king summoned the tinsmith for an audience with him at the palace. The king had long mused over how the tinsmith managed his curious escape from the prison cell.

When quizzed by the king on exactly how he had escaped the seemingly unescapable cell, the tinsmith replied with a wry smile, "It is, your highness, a question of patterns, and patterns within patterns. Perhaps you might call these designs also." The tinsmith continued, "My wife is a weaver by profession, she designs rugs, mats, and carpets, weaving patterns into the wefts and the warps of her fabric. Also, by design, she happened upon the designer of the cell door, which held me in prison, and also by design, she acquired the design of the lock."

The king looked on in amazement as the tinsmith continued his story. "She then skilfully wove the lock design into the prayer mat which she made for me. The moment I prayed for the first time, I knew the design of the lock instantly.

With all of this, all I needed was some very small basic tools and different metals. From the discarded elements I designed for the guards, I was eventually able to design and make myself a key. With this key, I unlocked the door, walked through, relocked the cell, and escaped into the night with my family."

The king jumped with delight, exclaiming the tinsmith to be the wisest, most wily character in the kingdom.

The tinsmith once again smiled gently before finishing his incredible tale of escape. "We are all born with a mind, Your Highness, but this mind does not come with instructions, and we must learn for ourselves if it is to become a powerful instrument. Sadly, many people never learn to use their brains to their full effectiveness. This is a pity because effective ways of using our brains can be taught and learned."

Finally, the tinsmith concluded, "Once we understand this, we can free ourselves from the enslavement, which creates our perceived limitations."

Credit: The Magic of the Metaphor, Nick James

Reflection: I often imagine Nelson Mandela when I recount this story on my courses. The human capacity to expand our thoughts beyond our geographical location and circumstance is truly remarkable. In the simplest form of abstraction of thought we are able to create a different world inside our minds. It is this human imagination that has transcended our species to the pinnacle of the animal world. When was the last time you allowed your creative imagination to expand past your current situation?

CHAPTER 95

Aristotle & The War Lord

"Bury my body, do not build any monument, keep my hands outside so that the world knows the person who won the world had nothing in his hands when dying."
– Alexander the Great

Many people today with an interest in Greek philosophy divide philosophy with a historical demarcation line. It is similar to the line in time that places events Before Christ (BC) and after his crucifixion, or 'Annon Domini' (AD). In philosophy, this temporal separation is called the Pre-Socratic and Post-Socratic eras. Socrates signified a glorious period in Athens when three of the greatest philosophers that ever lived were influenced by each other. In a succession of handovers, similar to the line of royalty to a throne, there was a lineage of greatness passed from teacher to student starting with Socrates, followed by Plato, who Aristotle then followed. Socrates, Plato, Aristotle, in that order; three of the titans of Greek philosophy.

What is occasionally overlooked is the student of Aristotle. Aristotle of Stagira was born in 384 BC and died in 322 BC. Known as 'the man who knew everything' and later just 'The Philosopher', Aristotle was a true titan of Greek philosophy and a fitting finale to the trilogy. He was considered a master in many disciplines such as biology, politics, metaphysics, agriculture, literature, botany, medicine, mathematics, physics, ethics, logic and theatre! In 343 BC Aristotle was summoned by the King of Macedonia, Philip II of Macedon, to tutor his young son, Alexander. By the time of Alexander's death in Babylon at the young age of thirty-two, he had created an empire that stretched from Macedonia to Egypt and Greece, and to parts of India. Dying mysteriously in 323 BC by either poisoning or malaria, Alexander was never defeated on the field of battle and was recorded in history as one of the finest military tacticians of all time.

Aristotle tutored Alexander for seven years until his ascension to the throne in 336 BC, which was the beginning of his famous conquests. There is little doubt of the influence of Aristotle on the young Alexander, cultivating the future king in all elements of philosophy, logic and reason. Alexander was renowned for carrying his books on all of his conquests. Being a studious reader of philosophy, he innately understood the importance of reasoned thought and logic on the battlefield, making him a true 'thinking' soldier. Aristotle believed that non-Greeks were 'barbarians'; he especially held a dim view of the Persians and most likely encouraged Alexander to also adopt this view of the non-Greek subspecies which demanded the rule of a more cultivated culture such as Greece. Like many of his generation, Aristotle would have been told the great war stories of the Battle of Marathon in 490 BC, the Persian invasion in 480 BC, and the famous Greek triumphs over the Persian invaders at Plataea and Salamis.

Once Aristotle returned to Athens in 335 BC, the teacher and his student continued to stay in touch as Alexander laid the foundations for his empire. In what appears a symbiotic relationship, Alexander returned the gift of knowledge from Aristotle by introducing Aristotelian philosophy as far as India, acting like a bee transporting the pollen farther than it could ever hope to spread unaided.

Alexander, on his deathbed in Babylon, famously made three final requests. Firstly, to be carried only by his physicians, to prove that doctors cannot heal you once your time of departure arrives. Secondly, to have the path to his grave strewn with gold and jewels, to prove that all of the riches accrued in life are meaningless at the end. Finally, he requested he be buried with his hands exposed and empty, to show that even the man who conquered the world left it with empty hands.

Reflection: What can we learn from Alexander's final moments? Perhaps he became a Stoic; he certainly describes some Stoic ideology at the very end.

CHAPTER 96

What Type of Mindset do You Have?

"If you are the smartest person in the room,
you are in the wrong room."
– Confucius

Dr Carol Dweck has dedicated her professional life to understanding the attitudes of students in relation to failure. After over thirty years of research, she wrote *The Times*' best-selling *Mindset: The New Psychology of Success* and has since become a world-leading authority in the field of human potential.

In its simplest terms, she noticed that there appeared to be two categories of student and depending on which category the student fell into, it would be a predictor of success. From studying thousands of children, Dr Dweck coined the terms 'Fixed Mindset' and 'Growth Mindset', which described the students' underlying beliefs about learning, intelligence and capability.

Students with a 'Growth Mindset' believe intelligence and talent are not fixed entities and can be developed with application. They believe that effort is the pathway to mastery, and mistakes are part of the learning journey. A person with a 'Growth Mindset' also views failure as an opportunity to reflect and learn; they embrace challenges and welcome feedback. Finally, this group observe other people's success as inspirational.

Students with a 'Fixed Mindset' believe intelligence and talent are fixed and cannot be developed. They develop learned helplessness in which effort is fruitless and not worthy of committing to. Unfortunately, they believe that failure defines them as a person and is embedded within their self-identity. They conceal their flaws through lack of confidence, avoid challenges, and ignore feedback, viewing it as a personal criticism. Students with a 'Fixed Mindset' view other people's success as threatening.

In one study, Dr Dweck set a series of challenges for ten-year-olds. Some students got excited by the challenge of not knowing how to complete the task and set about solving what was in front of them; they saw it as a wonderful opportunity. Other students in the same class saw the same challenges as a threat and felt exposed because they did not know how to complete the tasks; they became defensive. They believed it was tragic and catastrophic and perceived the entire task as a judgement of their inabilities. Even more fascinating than this is what happened next. In one study, the 'Fixed Mindset' students openly admitted they would prefer to chat than study to pass if they were tested again. In another study, after failure, they looked to identify someone who had performed worse than they did, so they could feel better by bathing in the shortcomings of those below them in performance.

The genuinely fantastic element of Dr Dweck's research is the understanding of the malleability of the brain and its incredible capacity to develop and grow, regardless of age or perceived limitations. Whether our beliefs are conscious or subconscious, they strongly affect what we want and whether we succeed in attaining it, whatever 'it' may be. Perhaps a lesson for us all in this is how we set about cultivating a 'Growth Mindset'.

Reflection: Within many of the chapters of this book, we have explored different perspectives of self-limited beliefs and thinking. Explore which mindset you believe describes you. Whichever it is, understand that you can start changing the way you think. Like with many elements of this book, the start point is self-awareness, and from this position, in everyday opportunities, there resides the chance to change and grow. Being less of the person you don't want to be, and more of the person you do want to be is more effortless than you perhaps perceive. I hope you're becoming more aware of this with each page.

CHAPTER 97

Socrates' Directions

"I am not an Athenian, nor a Greek,
but a citizen of the world."
– Socrates

On a hot summer's day in ancient Greece, Socrates sat on a wall in the countryside, not far from Athens. The philosopher sat patiently musing philosophical thoughts and eating slowly from a bowl of olives prepared by his wife, Xanthippe.

The road that lay in front of Socrates connected Athens with Corinth to the east, roughly two days walk from city to city. From the direction of Corinth, a single traveller walked and approached Socrates. "Wise man, can you tell me the directions to the Agora in Athens, and can you counsel me of the people I will find there?"

Socrates, being Socrates, responded with a question, "Of course, kind sir, but first, please do tell from which province do you travel and what kind of people you leave behind?"

The traveller responded, "I travel from Corinth and am sad to leave this city. I have many friends, and Corinth's people are amongst the kindest, most honest, and considerate people a man could hope to encounter. I leave with a heavy heart but have hope of who awaits in Athens."

Socrates smiled gently and responded, "Good sir, follow this road until you reach a junction, turn left, and this road will take you to the centre of Athens. You shall see the Agora in the shade of the Parthenon. I will gladly tell you that the people from Athens sound so very similar to those you leave behind in Corinth."

For the next few hours, Socrates carried on his day, mainly comprised of sitting on the wall, eating olives, and contemplating the universe's puzzles. Once again, a traveller approached the philosopher from the direction of Corinth. "Wise man, can you tell me the directions to the Agora in Athens, and can you counsel me of the people I will find there?"

Socrates, being Socrates, responded with a question, "Of course, kind sir, but first, please do tell from which province do you travel and what kind of people you leave behind?"

The traveller responded, "I travel from Corinth and am happy to leave that city behind. I have left because the city is full of beggars and thieves; you need to keep your wits about you in Corinth for the people cannot be trusted. I leave, however, with hope in my heart and in search of more trustworthy and loyal friends in Athens."

Socrates smiled gently and responded, "Good sir, follow this road until you reach a junction, turn left, and this road will take you to the centre of Athens. You shall see the Agora in the shade of the Parthenon. I must counsel you caution when arriving in Athens: I think you will find the people from Athens very similar to the ones you leave behind in Corinth."

Reflection: The world today appears at times to be more divided than at any time in memory. 'Fake news' seems to be driving wedges between left and right, conservative and liberal, Christian and Muslim, as well as climate change activists and climate change deniers. Each news-fuelled group, consumed by their cognitive biases and unable to see the widening chasm of common ground, seem to be digging the trenches of separation further. We are all citizens of Earth, and perhaps learning from the philosophers of antiquity can help us remember that!

CHAPTER 98

Legacy

"I think, therefore I coach."
– Phil Quirk

I have waited until the very final chapters to explore the book's title. In truth, it took me to this point to replace 'Untitled' with the one you have in your hand. I had always suspected that the title would reveal itself when the time was appropriate, in a kind of 'when the student's ready, the teacher will appear' type philosophy.

Philosophy has given me so much, personally, educationally, spiritually, and professionally. I had once considered philosophy to be the dominion exclusively of the intellectual. Little did I know that reading philosophy would mean more than sitting beneath an oak tree reciting long undecipherable passages of text, contemplating the meaning of my existence. It would be applicable to my everyday life and furnish me with ideas and knowledge that quickly improved my perspective on life. Learning philosophy subsequently extended into my professional coaching practice and underpinned my professional approach with my clients. All I can ever hope for with my coaching is to provide the very questions that encourage a person to explore their thoughts and new conclusions.

Sometimes this is very successful, other times it is not.

Early in my coaching career, I used to get all bent out of shape when clients weren't making the 'progress' I hoped they would. It took several years and many successes and failures to understand that the only person who can really effect change is the person themselves. Once I had learned this significant lesson of causation it allowed me to see things from a new perspective. I now understand that my role was not as an agent of change as much as a facilitator of opportunities to change.

All I can hope for is to encourage the person to 'cogito ergo mutatio' – 'I think therefore I change'.

Whether you access the teachings of Socrates, Plato's *The Republic* and *Allegory of the Cave*, Zeno's first wave of Stoicism, or read about Eratosthenes measuring the world using a papyrus text, geometry, and a stick, you can learn from all of these great minds. If you are curious to learn more about the individual work of any of these philosophers of antiquity, I urge to fuel that fire with a more detailed exploration of their works.

Socrates wisely espoused one hot summer's afternoon in the Agora, *"I cannot teach anybody anything; I can only make them think."*

Cogito Ergo Mutatio

CHAPTER 99

Philosophy in The Future

"Those who cannot remember the past are condemned to repeat it."
– George Santayana

I truly believe that never before in modern history has antiquity's wisdom been as relevant as it is today. We have evolved to become information-rich and wisdom poor, and in doing so, we are in danger of forgetting the lessons learned from our ancestors. As a father it saddens me to look around the world and see the inequality and injustice that exists in our modern society. While this book is by no means a political statement, I cannot pretend it is not a philosophical judgement on modern society.

If a strong monkey were to hoard all of the available bananas, far in excess of the amount needed to satiate his appetite, and in doing so, prevented the other weaker monkeys from accessing food, we would judge this behaviour for what it is – greed; behaving in a way that would force the majority to go without anything, so the minority could have everything.

We would study this monkey's behaviour to understand what is wrong with it. It would appear within our species that similar behaviour is rewarded with acclaim and a place on the cover of *Forbes* magazine.

By writing this book, I hope to encourage you to absorb some philosophical and Stoic principles into your life. Learn from Socrates' humble wisdom, commit to your personal Agoge, and develop resilience and fortitude. Finally, appreciate the knowledge left for us by the many wonderful thinkers and philosophers that we succeeded in history.

For large parts of human evolution, we have used storytelling and metaphors to teach, grow, and develop, while also ensuring lessons are learned. This means we are not doomed to repeat the mistakes of those who came before us. Whether these stories are myth or fact is irrelevant; the underlying meaning of the metaphor has always been vital for our continued development.

The mysterious story of Atlantis should serve as a warning against the hubristic direction of our modern civilisation. Whether the story is an actual historical event, or a metaphor for the utopian society Plato describes in *The Republic*, the lessons can still be drawn. Plato describes Atlantis through the character of Critias in his dialogues.

Located just past the Pillars of Hercules (generally assumed to mean the Strait of Gibraltar), Atlantis was larger than both Libya and Asia Minor (Turkey). Technologically advanced, the people of Atlantis were blessed with wealth, precious jewels and abundance beyond any civilisation that had come before them. According to the story, the Sea God Poseidon, created Atlantis. Poseidon fell in love with a mortal woman called Clieto who lived on some islands. When her parents passed away, they married and had five sets of male twins. The eldest of the first set of twins was named Atlas and would become the first Atlantean king. We can thank Atlas' name for the Atlantic Ocean, the Atlas Mountains, and of course Atlantis itself. According to Hesiod's *Theogony*, Atlas was one of the strongest gods. His punishment for choosing to side with Cronus and the Titans against Zeus and the Olympians in the ten year war between the gods was to forever bear the weight of the heavens on the western edge of the world.

Atlantis was a beautiful city comprising of alternating concentric circles, three of water and two of land. At the centre of Atlantis was the heart where the Atlanteans built a citadel and holy temple with gold and silver, dedicated to Poseidon and Clieto. Streams of tepid water and cold spring water circulated throughout the city and provided the people of Atlantis with all the resources they needed to create a thriving culture. In the beginning, the citizens appreciated their good fortune with grace and humility. However, over time they forgot their place and became greedy and arrogant, diluting their virtuous state and dishonouring their gods. For this impiety, they were judged and found wanting, then punished for their indiscretions without mercy.

Plato writes that Critias was told the story of Atlantis by his grandfather, who had been told it directly by the Athenian statesman, Solon (one of the Seven Sages of Greece). Solon himself had learned the mysterious story of Atlantis from an Egyptian priest, who placed the time very specifically at 9,000 years prior (because we can accurately identify Solon's time at 600 BC, we can assume the approximate time to be 9,600 BC). This is fascinating because the date places the possible event in history at a time called the 'Younger Dryas Event'. This was a 'mini' ice age lasting around 1,100 years which started, and ended, abruptly as the planet was exiting its last glacial period. Triggered by the violent change in global ocean temperatures, there would most certainly have been events of Biblical flooding and other natural disasters such as earthquakes and possible tsunamis.

Through the mouth of Critias, Plato describes the arrogance and hubris that had manifested itself over time within the people of Atlantis. Whether Plato was writing this as a warning for the people of Athens in the 2nd century BC using the mystical metaphor of the collapse of Atlantis or, if Atlantis was an accurate account of a lost civilisation during a time of undoubted naturally occurring events from the 'Younger Dryas', we can never be certain.

We can be certain of the lessons that we can draw from the story though.

Reflection: Around the world today there is evidence we are forgetting the mistakes made by previous generations. While I entirely believe in looking forwards in life, that does not preclude both reflection and history aiding me in navigating my vessel through the passage of time. Learning the wisdom from those who came before us is a shortcut to wisdom itself. We mustn't allow our biggest mistakes to repeat themselves with our future generations.

But what we can we do individually?

Well, simply stated, your mind is quite incredible, and the entire focus of this book is written to enable you to stand on the shoulders of the genius minds that have walked before you. I hope from these pages you have found value in the ideas we have explored together. There is nothing new in these 99 chapters; in truth, very little knowledge is truly virgin. Most of today's ideas, whether in science, philosophy, mathematics, or literature, are modified and reinvented concepts that have come before them. It matters not that these ideas are 2,400 years old, it only matters that there is value within the words on these pages to evolve your thinking, change your habits, improve your mindset, and establish a firmer grasp on the direction of your life.

If we have done any of these things, then I think the entire project will have been a success.

I exchanged some of my time to write this book, and I consider this exchange one of the wisest investments of time in my life. I hope your exchange of time to read this book is also an investment you deem to be of sound judgement. We are all custodians of our allocation of time. Whatever the number of matches expended to read this book, I hope the investment return was worthwhile.

Phil

Bibliography

Aurelius, M., (2006) **Meditations.**

Beck, D., (2005) **Spiral Dynamics: Mastering Values, Leadership and Change**.

Brule, D., (2017) **Just Breathe: Mastering Breathwork for Success in Life, Love, Business, and Beyond.**

Camus, A., (2005) **The Myth of Sisyphus: Penguin Great Ideas.**

Carney, S., (2020) **The Wedge: Evolution, Consciousness Stress, and the Key to Human Resilience.**

Clear, J., (2018) **Atomic Habits: An Easy and Proven Wa Build Good Habits and Break Bad Ones.**

Dass, R., (2019) **Becoming Nobody.**

De Sena, J., Et al., (2018) **The Spartan Way: Eat Better. Better. Think Better. Be Better.**

Epictitus., (1701) **Enchridion.**

Epitcituts., (2008) **Discourses and Selected Writings.**

Gelb, M., (2009) **Think Like Da Vinci: 7 Easy Steps Boosting Your Everyday Genius.**

Grof, S., Grof, C., et al., (2010) **Holotropic Breathwork: A New Approach to Self-Exploration and Therapy.**

Hof, W., Et al., (2012) **Becoming the Iceman: Pushing Past Perceived Limits.**

Holiday, R., et al., (2016) **The Daily Stoic: 366 Meditations on Wisdom, Perseverance, and the Art of Living.**

James, M., Jongeward, D., (1996) **Born To Win.**

Junger, S., (2017) **Tribe: On Homecoming and Belonging.**

Kahneman, D., (2012) **Thinking, Fast and Slow.**

Kolb, B., Gibb, R., (2011) **Brain Plasticity and Behaviour in the Developing Brain.**

Kolk, B., (2019) **The Body Keeps The Score: Mind, Brain nd Body in the Transformation of Trauma.**

guire, E., Gadian., D, Ingrid S., Johnsrude., Christopher (2000) **Navigation-related structural change In the hip- mpi of taxi drivers.**

eown, P., (2015) **The Oxygen Advantage: The simple, scientifically proven breathing technique that will revolutionise your health and fitness.**

Mitchell, S., (1988) **Tao Te Ching.**

Nagoski, E., et al (2019) **Burnout: The Secret to Solving the Stress Cycle.**

Nestor, J., (2021) **Breathe, The New Science of a Lost Art.**

Owen, N., (2001) **The Magic Of The Metaphor: 77 Stories for Teachers, Trainers and Therapists.**

Plato., (2007) **The Republic.**

Plato., (2017) **The Last Days of Socrates: Euthphro, Apology, Crito and Phaedo.**

Pransky, J., (2011) **Somebody Should Have Told Us!: Simple Truths for Living Well.**

Robertson, D., (2019) **How to Think Like a Roman Emperor: The Stoic Philosophy of Marcus Aurelius.**

Rovelli, C., (2021) **Helgoland.**

Seneca., (2004) **Letters From a Stoic: Epistulae Morales Ad Lucilium.**

Tonkov, G., (2019) **Feel to Heal: Releasing Trauma Through Body Awareness and Breathwork Practice.**

Tushkan, G., (1994) **The Hunter of the Pamirs: A Novel of Adventure In Soviet Central Asia.**

Winchester, R., (2009) **The Professor and the Madman: A Tale of Murder, Insanity, and the Making of the Oxford Dictionary.**